THE SMARTEST WOMAN NEVER, *EVER* SAYS . . .

- *All men are the same.* (The Smartest Woman knows that men like women who build bridges, not walls.)
- *He's a nice guy, but he's not my physical type.* (The Smartest Woman knows that husband material looks like human material.)
- *I want you to know* everything *about me.* (Men like women who reveal their sexual history on a need-to-know-basis.)
- *Will I hear from you tomorrow?* (The Smartest Woman never treats any date as though it's her last.)
- *How will I live without you?* (The Smartest Woman never treats any relationship as though it's her last.)
- *I'll forgive you . . . this time.* (The Smartest Woman knows that it's *never* smart to settle for less than you deserve.)

UNCOVER THE REAL SECRET
TO FINDING, KEEPING, AND MAKING
THE MOST OF ANY RELATIONSHIP, IN . . .

MEN LIKE WOMEN
WHO LIKE THEMSELVES
(And Other Secrets That
the Smartest Women Know)

Also by Steven Carter & Julia Sokol

HE'S SCARED, SHE'S SCARED

WHAT SMART WOMEN KNOW

MEN WHO CAN'T LOVE

WHAT REALLY HAPPENS IN BED

Men Like Women Who Like Themselves

(And Other Secrets
That the Smartest Women Know)

Steven Carter & Julia Sokol

A DELL TRADE PAPERBACK

A DELL TRADE PAPERBACK

Published by
Dell Publishing
a division of
Bantam Doubleday Dell Publishing Group, Inc.
1540 Broadway
New York, New York 10036

The trademark Dell® is registered in the U.S. Patent and
Trademark Office.

ISBN 0-440-50615-8

Reprinted by arrangement with Delacorte Press

Printed in the United States of America
Published simultaneously in Canada

July 1997

10 9 8 7 6 5 4 3 2 1
BVG

For Jill,
one of the
Smartest Women we know.

Men Like Women
Who Like Themselves

The Smartest Woman Knows a Lot About Men, But She Knows Even More About Herself.

Who are "the smartest women"? Are they women with Mensa-meriting IQs? Are they women with superior educations, or fabulous careers? Are they women who know how to play the stock market, how to make a great crème brûlée from scratch, or how to put up drywall? Our answer is none of the above.

The Smartest Woman is a woman who has a clear, indisputable sense of her worth and her power. She knows what she brings to a relationship, and she knows what she deserves in return. The Smartest Woman knows how to meet and survive difficult challenges; she also knows how to "tend the field" during gentler times. The hard work of relationships is rewarded because she is getting back as much as she puts in. In simple terms, the Smartest Woman knows and respects who she is. Because of this inner knowledge, she is in control of herself and her life.

Sometimes it feels as though it would be wonderful to discover that it's all a big trick done with mirrors. It would be strangely comforting to discover that these very same smart women stuff themselves with gooey chocolates and ice cream when nobody is looking, break dishes, cry in their walk-in closets, and correspond day and night with mail-order therapists through secret post office boxes. But they don't.

It's enough to make you jealous and resentful as hell. But you know many of these women, and you like many of these women. Some are your friends, some are your neighbors, some are your relatives, and some—dare we say it—are even your mothers. So if you can't hate these women or pretend they don't exist, what can you do with them? Well, for starters, you can admire them. Then, you can find out their secrets.

The Smartest Woman understands the men in her life. In the truest sense, she knows who these men are and what's important to them. She understands that when it comes to relationships, there are things men like and there are things men don't like. Very specific, very serious, and very meaningful things that have little to do with the superficial issues such as hair color, nose shape, or breast size. It's essential for women to have this information and to take it to heart.

THE SMARTEST WOMAN KNOWS . . .
Men Like Women Who Like Themselves.

THE SMARTEST WOMAN KNOWS . . .

If you want to be successful in your personal life, you have to "come to your senses."

You need:

- A sense of balance
- A sense of worth
- A sense of values
- A sense of priorities
- A sense of self
- A sense of humor

THE SMARTEST WOMAN KNOWS . . .

. . . How to Take Care of Herself Without Sacrificing Her Partnerships.

. . . How to Take Care of Her Partnerships Without Sacrificing Her Soul.

Many women ask the same question: "Why should a smart woman care about what men like, want, and need?" The truth is that women care about what men like because they are women, just as men care about what women like because they are men. Don't worry: caring about what men like and want doesn't automatically turn you into a throwback from the fifties.

You see, all evidence to the contrary, men and women are not really from different planets. In many ways they are far more alike than they are different. They share the same kinds of basic needs and vulnerabilities. And they both want to give and receive love. The way this is expressed may be different. The way it is handled may be different. But the humanness is the same.

Figuring out what men want is more about communication than it is about differences. It is more about sameness than it is about separateness. It's more about finding common ground than it is about waging turf wars. And it is more about listening than it is about caretaking.

THE SMARTEST WOMAN KNOWS . . .

Men need to learn to listen to women; women need to learn to listen to men; and all of us need to learn to listen to our inner voices, which are sometimes the clearest voices of all.

THE SMARTEST WOMAN KNOWS . . .

Everyone struggles with relationships, and there are *no* exceptions to that rule.

- It doesn't matter how much money you have (ask Ivana Trump).
- It doesn't matter how much fame you have (ask Roseanne).
- It doesn't matter how intelligent you are (ask Gloria Steinem).
- It doesn't matter how gifted you are (ask Nadia Comaneci).
- It doesn't matter how well you know a U.S. president (ask Gennifer Flowers).
- It doesn't matter if you are vivacious (ask Oprah), voluptuous (ask Loni Anderson), or drop-dead gorgeous (ask Julia Roberts).
- It doesn't matter how many times you've been married (ask Elizabeth Taylor), how many magazine covers you have graced (ask Iman), or how much you know about sex (ask Dr. Ruth).
- It doesn't even matter if you're a relationship expert (just ask us).

THE SMARTEST WOMAN KNOWS . . .

Rocket Ships to the Moon Get There in Stages. Why Should It Be Any Different for Relationships?

We need to get one thing straight before we go any further. When you talk about relationships, you have to talk about the stages of a relationship. You wouldn't start a novel on page 100, you wouldn't start a dinner with a piece of pecan pie, and you wouldn't start a race ten yards before the finish line. No matter how anxious you are to have 2.3 kids and live happily ever after, you have to realize that a real relationship is an exercise in growth. A real relationship is a process of getting to know someone and letting yourself be known. It means developing mutual trust, mutual respect, and mutual intimacy. It means moving toward genuine commitment, and it means moving slowly and carefully.

THE SMARTEST WOMAN KNOWS . . .

What works in a ten-year-old relationship isn't going to work on the first date.

What seemed cute on a first date isn't necessarily endearing two years later.

———— ❦ ————

Even FedEx can't deliver a good relationship overnight.

Stage One
Getting to Know You

Myth: It was "love" at first sight.
Fact: Spell it l-u-s-t. Sometimes it lasts. Too often it doesn't.

THE SMARTEST WOMAN KNOWS . . .

No matter *how* powerful the attraction, no matter *how* unique the chemistry, and no matter *how* promising the potential, getting to know another human being is a process that can't be rushed.

THE SMARTEST WOMAN KNOWS . . .
Finding and Maintaining Long-term Love Requires Big-time Work.

Every year, dozens of new books are published about relationship issues. Every month, dozens of women's magazines devote page after page to these same questions. At 31, Dawn feels as though she has read most of those books and magazines. And whenever Oprah has a show that seems particularly interesting, Dawn's mother tapes it and sends it to her by mail. The fact is that Dawn is embarrassed to admit how much time she has already spent trying to figure out how to get one specific man—or men in general—to like her. But so far, paying all this attention to how she looks, what she says, or how she acts hasn't gotten her what she wants. That's not to say men don't find Dawn attractive and appealing. They do. But she's had too many first dates that didn't turn into second dates, too many second dates that didn't turn into third dates, too many third dates that didn't turn into relationships, and too many relationships that unraveled all too soon.

Dawn desperately wants a satisfying, fulfilling long-term relationship. She wants children, and she wants to be part of a family. But in order to do that she needs a mate, and since her sexual orientation is heterosexual, this means she is going to have to relate to men. This fact is sometimes enough to make her want to scream.

What Dawn really wants is a miracle. She wants a relationship to be easy, and she wants it to be fast. But relationships don't work that way. At least not the kind of relationships that work.

Many women think like Dawn. They say: "He's a man; I'm a woman; we're attracted to each other. Shouldn't the rest be easy?" Well, sometimes it is, but just as often the relationship never gets off the ground, and all that's left is the memory of a bad date, or just a bad moment that ends the possibility of any future dates. Granted, not all relationships are made in heaven. Try as we might—and often we try way too hard—some relationships are simply not meant to be.

But what about the many relationships that, given half a chance, could turn into something special? What happens to all of those couplings that seem so ripe with potential but fall through the cracks so quickly? What about all those could-be-compatible relationships that stall or lose their way moments out of the starting gate? So many promising beginnings come to such abrupt endings. So many potentially great relationships end up on the cutting-room floor.

Beginnings are hard. When two strangers meet, they have too little history to keep them stuck together through thick and thin. One or two steps "out of bounds" for either party and everything quickly becomes unglued. When we first meet, very few of us have the foresight or judgment to give each other a real chance. It seems like everyone has a hair trigger. One false step, one wrong move, one missed cue, and either member of that would-be relationship thinks, "I'm out of here," and all that potential is history.

Women have to be particularly careful about making the wrong kind of quick judgments, because often the only men who don't say or do something wrong are the ones who are frightfully skilled at beginnings. These are the professional daters, the ones who make no mistakes. These men always say the right thing, and always do the right thing. At least at first. The only mistake is yours, for being taken in by all that smoothness.

Men often make similar mistakes in the beginning. They are frequently enchanted by women who are fearless about saying and doing the kinds of things that every man wants. And they can turn away from sincere women who are not as practiced at seduction.

Every beginning is richly laced with ritual and fantasy. It's a necessary part of the process, and if there is too great a shortage of either one, the energy tends to fade quite quickly and interest wanes. But as complex, as demanding, and as draining as these beginnings are, they are still just beginnings. And if you are fortunate enough to get a good spin of the dice and advance past the first square, you can be assured that even greater challenges await you.

Beginnings are exciting. Beginnings are scary. Beginnings are fun. They are also confusing, sometimes embarrassing, and all too often disappointing. Yet, as difficult as it may be at times, courtship is a process that must be endured by many evolved species, and human beings are no exception. And endure we do. No sooner have you sworn off dating forever and ever and ever and ever than you find yourself once again playing nervously with the ice cubes in your sparkling water as you look into the eyes of a virtual stranger, wondering if maybe, just maybe, this could be "the one."

It certainly is possible. But maybe this could be something else. Maybe this man will be a new friend, perhaps even a best friend. Maybe this will be a great guy to introduce to someone else. Maybe this will turn into a terrific business opportunity. Maybe this will be a summer romance. Maybe this will be only a fun date, or someone to invite to your parties as a single man. Maybe this *will* be the one. Who knows?

The Smartest Woman would advise Dawn and others like her that they need to be thinking about ways to create opportunities and open up possibilities. They have to stop thinking about the marriage and babies that could happen in the future and start thinking about the dating and male friendships that could be happening right now.

THE SMARTEST WOMAN KNOWS . . .
The First Step in Finding a Long-term Relationship Is Developing a Realistic Attitude.

Men Like Women Who Know the Difference Between Myth and Fact.

Myth: It was "love" at first sight.
Fact: It was *dark*. In the beginning you can't always see what you need to see. Especially if either one of you is good at camouflage.

Myth: It was "love" at first sight.
Fact: It was longing. We all have empty spaces inside that long to be filled. But not every filling is good for your heart.

Myth: It was "love" at first sight.
Fact: It was convenient. You've reached that point in your life when you feel ready to settle down. But just because he is the first one to show up doesn't mean he should automatically get the prize.

Myth: It was "love" at first sight.
Fact: It was appropriate. He had all the credentials (but that's all he had). Your parents were thrilled (but it's not their life). You need a relationship, not a résumé.

Myth: It was "love" at first sight.
Fact: It was lobster. He spent big bucks and it

knocked you out. Sometimes it's easier
to pay your own way.

The Smartest Woman Always Keeps at Least One Foot Firmly Planted on the Ground.

At the Beginning of a Relationship, the Smartest Woman Knows How to Stay Awake.

When she's getting to know a potential love interest, the smartest woman stays . . .

• *Cautious*

Just because you care about what men like doesn't mean you should ever forget what you want and need. When you meet a new man, you have no way of knowing—no matter how charming or wonderful he may appear—whether he is truly good for you. So don't fall in love too quickly, don't fall into bed too quickly, and keep all your self-protective antennae in place. Your heart and your life are very precious. Give them the care they deserve.

• *Considerate*

Think about everyone's feelings—his and yours. Think about everyone's insecurities—his and yours. Think about everyone's sensitivities—his and yours. Be kind—to him, as well as to yourself.

• *Conscious*

When it comes to love, too many of us lapse into total illusion, delusion, and fantasy. Sometimes when we think we are falling in love with a person, we're really falling in love with love. Don't let yourself get so swept away that you can't tell the difference between love and lust, love and neediness, love and insecurity, love and image issues, love and money issues, love and status issues, or love and loneliness.

• *Clear*

The Smartest Woman always stays true to her own bottom line. She is who she is, and she doesn't want to behave in ways that compromise her essential self. She also knows what she really needs and she knows how to present those needs in ways that are both honest and straightforward.

THE SMARTEST WOMAN KNOWS . . .

You don't need a psychic to tell you what's good for you; you just need to pay attention.

Myth: All Men Are Jerks.

Fact: All Men Are Not Jerks, Just Like All Life-guards at the Beach Aren't Blond. It's Just the Jerks Who You Always Remember.

THE SMARTEST WOMAN KNOWS . . .

Men like women who don't think that the male of the species is an alien life-form.

Whether you're getting ready for an evening at home with your husband, a meeting with male co-workers, or an exciting first date, you're not preparing for a close encounter with an extraterrestrial. If you're going to build a relationship with a man, you have to know more about him. When you do, you'll discover that most of his likes, dislikes, needs, and wants are very similar to yours. So take off the yellow anticontamination suit, the decoder ring, and the overpriced moon boots. Put down your Phaser. And try to meet and understand the "other" sex in a way that makes you feel more like equals than opposites.

THE SMARTEST WOMAN KNOWS . . .

If you think men and women are from different planets, you need a stronger telescope.

If you think all men are the same, you need a stronger microscope.

THE SMARTEST WOMAN KNOWS . . .
Men like women who build bridges, not walls.

Recently Ted, 33, went out on a date with a woman named Maria. Ted thought Maria was spectacularly beautiful, and he was very interested in getting to know her better. But the negative comments she kept making about men were so brutal that Ted started to feel annoyed. Another woman might look at Maria and realize that what she wants from the man she's with is reassurance, but Ted didn't hear her vulnerability. All he heard was her hostility. Ted says he is getting fed up with the way women put men down. Lately he feels as though every woman he meets says something about men that he considers an absolute turnoff. Here are some of these fatal sentences:

- All men are babies.
- Men are only interested in sex.
- Men are only interested in football.
- Men are only interested in hanging out with their buddies.
- Men are more interested in making money than they are in making a family.
- Men never listen to what women say.
- Men don't talk.
- Men can never talk about their feelings.
- All men need to be trained.

When Ted was younger and a woman he liked made negative generalizations about men, he was inclined to try to prove himself. He wanted her to believe he would be different. Now when he hears one of these phrases, he goes into immediate withdrawal. He feels that women who use this kind of all-purpose put-down are themselves somewhat insensitive and shallow.

He says that when he thinks about a woman he wants to spend time with, he wants to be sure that she doesn't automatically discount his feelings. As a guy, he recognizes that men are often conditioned to bury their pain and hurt. However, that's not really how he wants to live the rest of his life. He wants a partner who is sensitive to that and understands that men have feelings too.

If you want to make generalizations about men, try some of these:

You get nervous, and he does too.
You have goals, and he does too.
You have dreams, and he does too.
You have flaws, and he does too.
You have needs, and he does too.
You get hurt, and he does too.
You have a personal history, and he does too.
You want to be understood, and he does too.
You want to be loved, and he does too.

Men Like Women Who Know the Difference Between . . .

. . . the man who plays tennis and the man who lives for tennis.

. . . the man who likes cars and the man who treats his car like a bride.

. . . the man who enjoys his work and the man who doesn't enjoy anything else.

. . . the man who owns a baseball glove and the man who sleeps at the ballpark.

. . . the man who watches football and the man who wants to decorate the house with AstroTurf.

. . . the man she's with and every other Tom, Dick, and Harry.

THE SMARTEST WOMAN KNOWS . . .

Whether You're Using a Modem to Connect to the Internet, or Dialing Out on Your Prized Princess Slimline, a Phone Call Is Just a Phone Call Is Just a Phone Call. . . .

About five seconds ago, Janelle's phone started to ring. It's Scott, the friend of a friend who's calling to make a blind date. Janelle, who has been expecting the call, is very comfortable, stretched out on the sofa, wearing a pair of baggy pants and a T-shirt, and drinking a diet soda. While Janelle is not exactly nervous, she's certainly aware that something is at stake in this phone call. According to her friend, Scott is "ready for something serious." Janelle is also ready for something serious. Is this fate, or what?

Janelle hopes she will like Scott, and she really hopes he will like her. So what should she say, and how should she say it? What does the Smartest Woman know about that all-important first contact with a new man?

• *The Smartest Woman recognizes the wisdom of keeping the first phone call short and sweet.*

Yes, we've all heard stories about people who met over the phone, spent hours talking, and then went on to live happily ever after. But long conversations with someone with whom you've never made eye contact can also be a prelude to disaster.

For example, if Janelle stopped and thought about it for a minute, she would remember Phil, her last blind date. She and Phil talked for hours on the phone the first time they spoke. Then, when they met, she wasn't at all attracted to him. Yet, because she had told him so much about herself and listened to so much about him, she felt obligated to go out with him several times. They were strangers with an intimate contact. This is how people who are all wrong for each other sometimes end up in a bad relationship.

Yes, it feels very comfortable sitting in your home environment, chatting on the phone. That's why this environment is conducive to establishing a false intimacy that comes all too quickly (and long before the real thing ever could). The Smartest Woman would tell you that when you and a new man first talk to each other, you need to be paying attention to a lot more than just the words. That is why you need to do it in a setting where you can get a better sense of his energy, his eye contact (or lack thereof), and his overall body language. This is also a way of protecting yourself from men who have learned how to "sell" themselves on the phone. The Smartest Woman knows that "phone chemistry" doesn't always translate into real chemistry.

• *The Smartest Woman doesn't use the phone to try to impress a man she's never met.*

In new situations, we sometimes try to say things

that give the impression that we're really terrific. You probably *are* really terrific, but trying to convey this on the phone can make a man think that you are too full of yourself, too hard to please, or perhaps too obviously insecure. The Smartest Woman knows that the most impressive people of all are those who don't try to impress anybody.

• *The Smartest Woman isn't too quick to be impressed by a man she's never met.*

Have you ever been to the movies and seen a trailer for a coming attraction that looks so incredible you can't wait to see the movie? When you finally get to see the actual film, you realize that every interesting moment was packed into that short preview, and there's not much else. Some men are like this. They are so practiced that they give you their greatest hits as soon as they meet you—but there's not much else. The Smartest Woman knows that you don't judge a movie by the coming attractions, and you don't judge a man by the first conversation, good or bad.

• *The Smartest Woman doesn't let herself be put on the defensive.*

Here's a rule: If some guy you barely know starts putting you on the defensive or asking you to prove yourself on the phone, don't do it. The Smartest Woman knows that if you start feeling defensive, it's probably because he's being offensive.

• *The Smartest Woman doesn't put a potential date on the defensive by grilling him for information about himself.*

Men hate it when women ask too many pointed, personal, information-gathering questions. They interpret this as a screening process, like a preliminary job interview. No fun! Grilling a chicken is one thing; grilling your date is another.

• *The Smartest Woman doesn't get drawn into sexual conversations that make her feel uncomfortable.*

Just because he puts it out there doesn't mean you have to pick it up. Someone who does this has typically established sex as his first priority. He needs to know right there, up front, that you are going to respond accordingly. Unless this is what you want, and the *major* thing you want, don't get involved. This is one of those games that is best stopped before you even roll the dice.

• *The Smartest Woman doesn't start sexual conversations with a stranger.*

Yes, you may want him to find you attractive, but this is not the way to bait your line. Just about every fish will bite on this one, including the trash fish. Just as important, for a well-intentioned man this can be as much of a turnoff as a turn-on. Besides, the Smartest Woman knows she is trying to make a human connection first, not a physical connection.

- *The Smartest Woman knows how to find something easy to talk about.*

Easy is the important word here. You don't want to weigh this conversation down with heavy material, particularly past traumas or future hopes. So keep it in the moment, keep it real, and keep it pleasant. Don't search exhaustively for common interests, powerful connections, or clear signs that this is going to be special.

The Smartest Woman Knows How to Make the Date, Tell Him She's Looking Forward to It, and *Get Off the Phone.*

THE SMARTEST WOMAN KNOWS . . .

Men Like Women Who Are So Confident of What They Have to Offer that They Never Have to Try Too Hard.

THE SMARTEST WOMAN KNOWS . . .
You're Not Going Anywhere if You Leave Yourself Behind.

Janelle and Scott have passed the preliminaries, and they are about to have their first real date. Janelle is looking forward to this, a lot. Scott sounds like an interesting man. Janelle can't wait to get to know him better, so for this date she's pulling out all the stops. She's been eating nothing but rabbit food for five days so that she'll look thin. She had her nails done; she shampooed her hair, using a new conditioner that was guaranteed to "improve the shine"; she shaved her legs, and she's covered her body in moisturizer because she's convinced no man wants a woman with dry, flaky skin.

Right now, Janelle is putting on a skinny little black dress that can't help but draw attention to those smooth, moisturized, expensively panty-hosed legs. But after all this effort, Janelle is still forgetting something. And it's not her deodorant. What is Janelle forgetting? In a word: Janelle.

Janelle has been so busy getting ready for her date with Scott that she has forgotten to stay connected to her essential self. What she needs to do is sit down, take a deep breath, and remind herself of who she is, what's important to her, and what she values.

Sure, getting ready for a date is fun and exciting, but all this excitement can make a ninety-nine-year-old woman behave like an immature fourteen-year-old. No matter what your age, suddenly the focus seems to be directed toward physical issues—the raging zit, the unwanted hair, or the visible stretch marks. The Smartest Woman knows that it's not smart to get completely swept up in the externals of how you look and where you'll be going. This kind of thinking can make you insecure and vulnerable. This kind of thinking can make you feel that your value depends on whether or not this man likes you. This kind of thinking can make you feel good if he's attracted to you, and bad if he's not. This is not smart, and it's not self-protective.

The Smartest Woman would tell you that you need to maintain your balance, even on a first date. If you're all caught up in externals, you're going to be unable to take in the really important information about him and his attitude toward life. You want to find out who he is, and just as important—in a nice, friendly way—you want to make it clear who you are.

The Smartest Woman Knows that She Always Wants to Be Remembered for Who She Is, Not How She Looks or What She's Wearing. She Always Checks In With Herself Before She Checks Herself Out In the Mirror and Heads Out the Door.

THE SMARTEST WOMAN KNOWS . . .
When You're Attracted to a Man, It's Easy to Lose Sight of What's Really Important.

That's why the Smartest Woman has a list of commandments to help her stay centered. Mary Clare is a really smart woman. Here's what she tells herself before, after, and sometimes even during every date.

Ten Dating Commandments for the Smartest Woman

1. My values are important to me, and I won't forget them, no matter how attractive he is.

2. I will stay centered and in control of my life, no matter how attractive he is.

3. I will not compromise my bottom line, no matter how attractive he is.

4. I will self-protectively pay attention to any of my doubts and concerns about him, no matter how attractive he is.

5. I will never jump in over my head, no matter how attractive he is.

6. I realize that fantasies keep me off balance, and I will not start spinning fantasies about the future, no matter how attractive he is.

7. If this doesn't work, it's because it's not supposed to work.

8. If this doesn't work, it's not because there's anything wrong with me.

9. If this doesn't work, there's still something I can learn from this experience.

10. If he seems too good to be true, he probably is.

THE SMARTEST WOMAN KNOWS . . .
Men Like Women Who Don't Botch Their Own PR.

You barely know him; perhaps you've only talked briefly. Yet you want to be reassured that superficial things aren't important to him. You want to be reassured that you won't be rejected for what you perceive to be your shortcomings. So the first thing you do is give him a résumé of your physical shortcomings. A wise strategy? We don't think so. Instead of noticing everything that's right about you, he may well start focusing on what you have told him is wrong about you. Things he may not even have noticed suddenly take center stage. And they can become as large to him as they seem to you.

It isn't your job to let a man know how "not perfect" you are. Especially since you have absolutely no idea what is or isn't important to him. Things that you think are dreadful may, to him, be insignificant. Or endearing. Or absolutely adorable. After you've known each other a decade or two, you'll find all this out. In the meantime, keep your insecurities to yourself.

———❦———

The Smartest Woman Doesn't Draw Attention to What She Perceives to Be Her Flaws.

She doesn't talk about . . .

. . . her latest wrinkle
. . . her latest blemish
. . . her imperfect nose
. . . her imperfect body
. . . her lack of style
. . . how much younger other women look
. . . how envious she is of obviously beautiful
women
. . . how ancient she feels
. . . how ancient she thinks she's starting to look
. . . how thin other women are
. . . how much weight she needs to lose
. . . how bloated she gets during her period.

Myth: A Good Relationship Should "Click" Right Away.

Fact: Too Many Women Confuse the "Click" of a Good Connection with the "Tick, Tick, Tick" of a Time Bomb That's Just Waiting to Go Off.

Two people can "click" for all the right reasons or all the wrong ones; and it's often very hard to tell the difference. In the beginning, there are more important sounds to be listening for, like the sounds of sincerity, of decency, and of genuine interest. Besides, for every story we've heard of relationships that "clicked" at the very beginning, we've heard just as many about relationships that took many months, or even years, to "suddenly click."

THE SMARTEST WOMAN KNOWS . . .

Men Like It When a Woman Has the Sense to Order Her *Own* Portion of French Fries—No Matter How Appealing *His* Look.

———❦———

The Smartest Woman Knows How to Keep the First Dinner from Turning into the Last Supper.

Vanessa and Joel are having dinner in the garden of a beautiful restaurant in southern California. Night is falling, there's a gentle sea breeze, and around the garden little white lights are twinkling. The setting is fairy-tale; the mood is Steven King. Joel and Vanessa have been sitting there for a little more than an hour, and Joel can't wait to leave. Vanessa is not having a happy effect on his digestive system, and all he can think about is the tension in his shoulders, and his sinking heart.

For starters, when the menu came, Vanessa vacillated for a full eight minutes, trying to decide between the grilled chicken breast with cilantro or the baked chicken breast with thyme and parsley. When the waiter asked Vanessa if she wanted a baked potato or rice, she said she didn't want a carb. Within seconds of uttering this statement, Vanessa started in on the bread basket. The waiter has filled it two more times, and now seems to be avoiding their table. As Vanessa grazes through the leftover crumbs, she is gazing longingly at Joel's baked potato in a way that Joel never ever remembers being looked at. All of Joel's survival instincts are urging him to secure the perimeter and guard his food.

Now, any woman knows that Joel is overreacting, but Joel doesn't know that Joel is overreacting. When he looks at Vanessa, he gets a glimpse of the unhappy future they might share if they ended up together. All he can see are painful years spent waiting for Vanessa to make up her mind, her ever-expanding waistline, and a final life-or-death struggle over the linguine.

Women don't realize it, but when men take them out to dinner for the first time, even the nicest guy in the world is likely to have his antennae fully extended, dissecting and interpreting every moment the same way psychologists dissect and interpret the answers to the Minnesota Multiphasic Personality Inventory. Something about the formal setup of a dinner date invites observation and analysis. So much seems to be at stake. It's like a minilaboratory with a myriad of issues laid bare for observation: money, sharing, interpersonal skills, table manners, decision-making ability, education, grooming, toilet habits, attitude toward time. Obviously, if a man is overly cautious and critical, there is nothing you can do about it. However, there is such a thing as being over the top.

The Smartest Woman Knows That Men Tend to Be Wary of Any Woman . . .

- who asks to change tables with an inexplicable sense of urgency.

- who starts complaining from the moment she sits down until the second she leaves (too hot, too cold, too drafty, too airless, too loud, too quiet, too slick, too trendy, too old-hat, too spicy, too bland, too boring).
- who sends back the wine for no apparent reason.
- who takes over the ordering—wine, entrée, dessert.
- who picks at her own food and devours his.
- who tosses her hair more than the chef tossed the salad.
- who never stops ogling the room and its occupants.
- who compares the restaurant (unfavorably) to all of her favorite places.
- who complains . . . and complains . . . and complains.
- who spends more time in the rest room than she does at the table.
- who runs to the phone to give a play-by-play report to her best friend, her mother, or the person who arranged the introduction.
- who takes or makes calls on her cellular phone.
- who orders only the most expensive things on the menu.
- who says she has no room for dessert, but orders

a chocolate cake *to go* to share with her room-mate, expecting her date to foot the bill.

- who talks nonstop about absolutely nothing.
- who barely speaks at all.
- who gets into arguments with the restaurant staff (waiter, waitress, busperson, maître d').
- who uses her chair to joust with the woman at the table directly behind her.
- who keeps sending food back to the kitchen, and then argues to get the bill reduced accordingly.
- who reveals her image issues by compulsively fiddling with her makeup, her manicure, or her clothing.
- who gets a spot on her clothing, spends the rest of the meal trying to remove it, and involves half the restaurant in her plight.
- who gets chattier with the people at the next table than she does with the man she's with.
- who tells the waiter to order for her.
- who reveals her issues with control by trying to readjust the entire restaurant to meet her needs (trying to rewrite the menu to suit her demands or asking the waiter to readjust the thermostat, the music, the air-conditioning, the light, the noises from the private party in the next room).
- who questions every ingredient as though she has life-threatening allergies.

The Smartest Woman Knows the Difference Between:

    . . . being fun and being frantic.
    . . . being nervous and being neurotic.
    . . . being herself and being over the top.

The Smartest Woman Saves Her Scariest Material for Halloween Costumes.

Myth: If a Man Is Really Interested, He'll Take You Out to Dinner on the First Date.

Fact: Food and Love Have Only One Thing in Common—They Both Have Four Letters.

Many, many men feel as though they have been burned too often by women who are more interested in a good meal than a good relationship. These men are far more likely to opt for coffee or a drink. On the other hand, a lot of men who have little interest in finding a meaningful relationship consistently take their dates to the best places in town because they know it makes them *look* like they are taking you very seriously. You need to pay less attention to the venue and the menu, and more attention to the quality and content of your first interaction. You also might want to consider paying your own way to start things off on a more equal footing.

The Smartest Woman Never, Ever, Walks Away from the Things That Make Her Special.

THE SMARTEST WOMAN KNOWS . . .

Men Like Women Who Look Like They Have Someplace to Go.

Joni is a woman with a very full life. She wants to be a serious painter, so that's how she spends much of her spare time. To make money, she has a job as a graphic artist. She has lots of friends who love her, and tons of interests. She likes music; she's a great dancer; she knows how to sail, ski, play tennis; and she's very interested in politics and what's going on in the world. However, if you met her with a man, you wouldn't know about any of this.

You see, Joni is a throwback to an earlier time. Twenty years ago, if you read many of the popular women's magazines, most likely you would have gotten the message that you were expected to build your life around a man. For a lot of complicated reasons, Joni is stuck in a world that existed when she was still a very young child.

Although Joni bills herself as a contemporary woman, emotionally she believes that she is supposed to drop everything for a man, and that's how she behaves. Meet her alone or with some women friends, and you meet an independent, dynamic person; meet her with a man, and you meet a dependent, retiring person. This is Joni's secret side. You get the feeling that once she is with a man, everything else about her life is negotiable and dispensable.

This dichotomy in Joni's nature has caused her a lot of trouble with men. Typically, men are attracted to the gregarious, multifaceted Joni they first meet. They like her because she seems so outgoing and creative. But after a very short time she turns into a different person, and sometimes, without understanding why, these same men lose interest.

THE SMARTEST WOMAN KNOWS . . .

·   If You Would Give It All Up Tomorrow to Be with the Man You Love, You're Not Thinking About the Day After Tomorrow.

——————

If You Don't Value Who You Are and What You Have to Offer, Don't Expect That Anyone Else Will.

——————

If You Are Seriously Prepared to Give It All Up for the Man You Love, You're Living in the Wrong Century.

The Smartest Woman Knows How to Say "No" Even When Her Body Is Screaming "Yes."

THE SMARTEST WOMAN KNOWS . . .
Men Like Women Who Aren't Afraid to Be Afraid of Sexual Intimacy.

Meredith is walking hand in hand with the tennis pro on the beach in Puerto Rico. It's the first night of the fantasy vacation she has been promising herself for the last two and a half years. It's perfection. Gentle sea breezes are blowing, stars are twinkling, and the surf is an inviting 75 degrees. The pro's name is Ryan. He's blond, blue-eyed, and six-foot-something, but who's measuring. Meredith is fairly certain that Ryan wants to go to bed with her. She becomes certain when *he suggests a dip in the ocean!!!!*

Fifteen years ago, Meredith might have ripped off her sarong in a minute, and who would have blamed her. But the Smartest Women know that times have changed, and they don't forget it.

———

Meanwhile, stateside, Meredith's friend Whitney is in an equally conflicting predicament. Whitney is on a first date with a startlingly terrific guy, and she can't quite believe that it's happening. They met for dinner at six, closed the restaurant, went to a coffee shop, and now are sitting on Whitney's couch.

Between the eye contact and the body language, Whitney feels as though she is about to faint. To make it even more unreal, she feels as though she's known him forever, and she never wants the evening to end. He has just pulled her close for a first kiss, and she never wants that to end either. Whitney knows there is one sure way to make sure that the evening doesn't end so soon. She also knows that unless she cools off the physical stuff very quickly, it's going to be very difficult not to go the distance.

Whitney and Meredith have slightly different situations. Whitney is fantasizing about a lifetime of shared dinners; Meredith is fantasizing about ten days of piña coladas and a ride to the airport. However, the issue on the table for both of them at this very moment is exactly the same: can anyone risk physical intimacy with a stranger?

We don't want to ruin Meredith's vacation, and we don't want to throw cold water on Whitney's marital fantasies. However, this is the truth:

> *No one can afford to have sex with a stranger, no matter how attracted you are to that stranger, no matter how much potential a relationship with that stranger may seem to have, no matter how good his references or his résumé. The fact is: a stranger is still a stranger.*

Meredith has to start thinking smart. Chances are, she's with a man who has walked this same beach on many perfect evenings, with many other women. If she looks carefully, she may even find some of his footprints from the previous night. Even if she has no emotional attachment or expectations, the rule for our times is: When you are sexually intimate with another person, you are automatically exposing yourself not only to him but to his history of exposure to STDs (sexually transmitted diseases).

Like her friend, Whitney has to consider all the health risks that might be involved. Even if she feels that she has known this man her entire life, she doesn't know the health-related details of his sexual history.

But Whitney has another issue as well. She may be exposing herself emotionally as well as physically. She doesn't know enough about this man, his values, or his intentions to jump into bed. She doesn't even know for sure whether he might like her better for *not* jumping into bed. The Smartest Woman wants to know a man long enough to have a fairly good idea how many previous partners he has had, how he treats his body, and how health conscious he is. She wants to know that intimacy means the same thing to him as it does to her, and she wants some assurance that when she finally does become sexually intimate with him, it is "safe" emotionally as well as physically.

He may be completely forthright and upright. He may have tested negative for every known STD. He may be crazy about you. He may be everything you've ever wanted in a man. He may be the cat's pajamas. He may be the king of England. But that still doesn't mean you have to sleep with him. You don't *have* to sleep with anyone until *you* are ready.

Sexual responsibility must go hand in hand with sexual freedom. More than anything else, the Smartest Woman knows that she is responsible to and for herself. This means that she wants to protect her health, her feelings, and her future. Sex changes a relationship, and it changes it very quickly. Make sure the relationship is strong enough to withstand those changes. And in the meantime, practice saying no.

The Smartest Woman Knows How to Say *No* Without Saying *Never.*

. . . She Isn't Afraid to Say "I'm Not Ready."

. . . She Isn't Afraid to Say "Not Yet."

. . . She Isn't Afraid to Say "We Need to Talk."

. . . She Isn't Afraid to Say "I Want to Know You Better."

. . . She Isn't Afraid to Say "I Want You to Know *Me* Better."

THE SMARTEST WOMAN KNOWS . . .
Men Like Women Who Don't Give Mixed Signals.

Not every man or woman can or should try to make beautiful music together. But sometimes it's hard to say that—particularly when the face staring at you from across the table looks as though it is feeling a chemistry that you're not sharing. Just because he thinks the two of you are a good match doesn't mean that you have to agree, or act as if you agree. Trying to protect his feelings by giving mixed signals is only going to get you in deeper, and it's only going to make him more confused. The Smartest Woman doesn't sit there acting like an angel when all she really wants to do is go home, *alone*.

The Smartest Woman Knows the Difference Between a Good-night Kiss and a Good-night Kissoff.

The Smartest Woman Knows She Can Embrace Her Sexuality Without Ever Feeling Pressured to Embrace a Stranger.

The Smartest Woman Is Never So Blinded by Lust that She Leaps Before She Looks.

THE SMARTEST WOMAN KNOWS . . .

No Matter How Many Times You Say "Are You Using Something?" You're Not Really Having a Conversation About Sex.

If you don't know a man well enough to talk about safe sex, then you don't know him well enough to have sex. You know this, and the average man knows it as well. Contrary to popular opinion, most men realize that every erection does not require immediate attention. They realize that these are troubled times, and that we all need to be cautious. More often than not, they don't know how to introduce the subject of safe sex. Remember: They're guys; they don't want to appear wimpy. More often than not, a man will be grateful to a woman who is centered enough and balanced enough to be self-protective in the sexual arena, because it's protecting him as well. In other words, talking about safe sex isn't going to make a good guy reject you.

This conversation about sex should take place while both of you are fully clothed, preferably in a place where neither one of you will be tempted to remove any clothing. Daylight hours and coffee shops are good choices. Here are some things that should be discussed: All sexual risks, including pregnancy and any sexually transmitted disease that either one of you can think of, including HIV, chlamydia, genital warts, herpes, syphilis, and gonorrhea.

Have either of you been exposed to any of these sexually transmitted diseases? If so, then you need to discuss the situation further with a medical doctor before having sex. If you haven't, then you still should talk to a doctor before beginning a sexual relationship. He may tell you that you need to make a commitment to practice safe sex and monogamous sex for at least six months. Then, before abandoning safe sex, it is advisable that you both visit physicians and get a clean bill of health, including a negative HIV test. We fully acknowledge that having this kind of conversation is awkward, uncomfortable, and unpleasant. And it may not be very romantic. However, it's absolutely necessary. And it's very smart.

The Smartest Woman Knows that She Doesn't Want to Become a Statistic. She Isn't Afraid to Say No to High-risk Sex.

. . . She Says *No* to Any Man Who Won't Discuss STDs.

. . . She Says *No* to Any Man Who Won't Discuss Birth Control.

. . . She Says *No* to Any Man Who Refuses to Wear a Condom.

. . . She Says *No* to Any Man Who Promises He'll "Pull Out in Time."

. . . She Says *No* to Any Man Who Is Sleeping with Other Women.

. . . She Says *No* to Any Man Who Is Sleeping with Other Men.

. . . She Says *No* to Any Man Who Won't Take an HIV Test.

. . . She Says *No* to Any Man Who Won't Disclose the Results of His HIV Test.

The Smartest Woman Never Says Yes Unless It's an Informed Yes.

THE SMARTEST WOMAN KNOWS . . .
Just Because You Said Yes in the Past Doesn't Mean You Can't Say No in the Present.

Karen has a problem. She's a sophisticated woman, but even when she wants to say no, she feels silly and childish doing so. Years ago, before she ever had sex, it was easier because she could tell men that she was a virgin. This seemed to be a valid excuse that everybody understood. Now she's no longer a virgin. So what's her excuse?

THE SMARTEST WOMAN KNOWS . . .
She Doesn't Need an Excuse to Say No to Sex.

THE SMARTEST WOMAN KNOWS . . .
There's a World of Difference Between a Night to Remember and a Man to Remember.

Just Because It Was a Night to Remember, He May Still Be a Man You Need to Forget.

The Smartest Woman Knows That a Man Likes a
Woman Who . . .

. . . Appreciates His Sensitivity Without De-
preciating His Sex Appeal.
. . . Notices His Biceps but Prefers His
Brain.
. . . Knows He's Not Superman and Doesn't
Hold It Against Him.

THE SMARTEST WOMAN KNOWS . . .
Men Like Women Who Appreciate the Beauty of Male Pattern Baldness.

Jennie's phone is ringing, and she's not sure she should answer it, because she knows who it is. It's Josh, a man she met at a party a few weeks ago. He's called a few times, and she's not sure what to do with him. A part of her keeps wishing that he would just go away, and a part of her likes talking to him. They have a lot in common, he makes her laugh, and he's very smart. So what's the problem? The problem is that he's far from a hunk. In fact, if anything, he may be a bit of a chunk.

You see, Jennie is worried about what people will think if she's seen with a man who doesn't radiate charisma and sex appeal. Jennie claims to want a long-term relationship with a solid guy. However, it isn't really clear whether Jennie would know a solid guy if she saw one.

What she needs to do is take a good look around and notice what solid guys look like. She needs to go look at the men who are shopping in supermarkets with their families, on golf courses with their friends, at restaurants with their wives, and at beaches, parks, or zoos with their children. Few of these men look as though they belong on the pages of *GQ* or *Esquire*. And Jennie needs to know that this is a good thing, not a bad thing.

THE SMARTEST WOMAN KNOWS . . .
Husband Material Looks Like Human Material.

You Can't Shop for a Relationship the Way You Shop for Groceries. But You Can Shop for a Relationship *While* You Shop for Groceries.

The Smartest Woman Knows that Men Like Women Who Know the Difference Between . . .

. . . Going on a First Date and Going to a Therapist.

. . . Going on a First Date and Going to an Encounter Group.

. . . Going on a First Date and Going to Confession.

When Lily thinks about long-term love, she thinks about a best friend, someone with whom she can share all her secrets. She wants to know that the man she's with will be totally accepting of who she is and how she feels.

Lily's idea of the perfect date is one in which she and her partner talk and talk and talk. If she likes a man, she wants him to know her, *really* know her. She wants to tell him about her insecurities and her anxieties. She wants to tell him about her problems with her mother, her attachment to her father, and the secret affair she had when she was eighteen with the married man who lived next door. After all, Lily thinks, how do two people get to know each other if they don't tell each other *everything*?

We agree that men and women who are committed to each other should also be committed to being "known" to each other. There is great comfort in this kind of familiarity; part of the process of creating intimacy means sharing things that you would not share with everyone else, or maybe anyone else. Here's the problem: When you've known a man for only a short time, it's inappropriate to share the inner workings of your psyche or your family, or the minute details of your biochemical cycles.

To the average man, these kinds of "premature" disclosures imply that you are either out to lunch or out of control. Granted, many men won't stop you from telling all there is to tell. Some won't stop you because they don't know how. (But just because they can't shut you down doesn't mean they don't shut down themselves.) Others may even encourage you, but what many of these guys may be doing is honing in on your vulnerability.

And yes, there are also a fair number of men who are equally guilty of this kind of inappropriate disclosure and may seem to be inviting you to respond in kind. *A word to the wise:* Men who do this are not necessarily inviting closeness. In fact, after a particularly revealing conversation or series of conversations, a man like this may run from his own oil spill. We call this the Exxon *Valdez* Syndrome.

With all this in mind, the Smartest Woman doesn't let herself become trapped in inappropriately intimate conversations too soon. We don't want to give the impression that these subjects are never to be talked about. They are all important. But not until the two of you know each other better . . . a lot better.

The Smartest Woman Knows There Are Some Things You Don't Discuss with a Man Until You Know Each Other Better. For Example:

- Your losing battle with PMS
- Your concerns about menopause
- Your recurrent yeast infections
- Your ex-boyfriend's violent temper
- Your sexual experimentations
- Your divorce
- Your issues with abuse
- Your eating disorders
- Your history in psychotherapy
- Your dysfunctional family structure
- Your history of alcohol or drug abuse
- Your medical history
- Your gastrointestinal tract
- Your overdrawn bank account, maxed-out credit cards, or any unpaid financial debts
- Your brother's (or any other family member's) frequent brushes with the law
- Your ongoing legal battles
- Your dabblings in occult sciences or witchcraft (unless it's an interest you both share)
- Your recent UFO abduction (unless you were abducted together)
- Your eight dachshunds, who share your bed
- Your eighteen cats, who share your everything

While all of these topics can make for interesting conversations, they will be a concern for many men. The truth is that everybody has controversial issues in his or her background. But when you pull these issues out during the first couple of meetings, you can seem out of control in all areas of your life. If this is what you talk about with somebody with whom there is no basis for trust, the typical man can't imagine what it is you tell someone you know really well. If you talk this way to a stranger, the typical man might not be able to imagine how there could ever be anything "special" and sacred between the two of you.

THE SMARTEST WOMAN DOESN'T . . .
. . . Treat Her Life like an Open Book, Although She's Willing to Share Some of the Pages.
. . . Treat Her Life like an Open Book Until She's Sure He Wants to Keep Reading.

THE SMARTEST WOMAN KNOWS . . .
Everyone Has Experienced Dates from Hell, but She Doesn't Want to Be Remembered as One of Them.

Do you remember many of your "bad" dates? Of course you do. Well, surprise, surprise—single men go through the same kind of experience. Let's look at some of them from the male point of view.

Marcus thought that Patricia sounded great on the phone. She likes scuba diving; he likes scuba diving. She likes tennis; he likes tennis. She wants to move away from the East Coast; he wants to move away from the East Coast. But on the date itself they were much less compatible. He says: "I have a new apartment that I'm pretty proud of, so I thought it would be fun if I invited her over for coffee on a Sunday afternoon to see it. In retrospect, I realize that she may have been annoyed that I didn't invite her out to dinner right off the bat, but I figured if we got along, we could go out to dinner after she saw my place.

"I spent a lot of time doing my own renovations, and so I gave her the grand tour. She didn't say a positive word about it. Not a word. When I showed her the kitchen cabinets that I did myself, all she could say was, 'I'd like them better if they were pickled.' Suddenly I found myself thinking that maybe I'd like her better if *I* got pickled.

"Maybe I'm overly sensitive, but I figured that if she didn't understand how hard I worked on my place, she wouldn't get anything about me."

———— ✦ ————

David met Alyssa at a large Christmas party, and he asked her out the first week in January—to go to a Friday night dinner party being given by a friend. The party was closer to David's house and since they were both coming from work, they agreed to meet at David's and take one car from there. David says:

"Sure, I noticed that during dinner she was sort of guzzling her wine, but she seemed perfectly fine and perfectly sober. When all the rest of us had coffee, I noticed she was still drinking wine. I figured maybe she was nervous, but then she got into an overly emotional argument with some guy over a movie that he hated and she loved, and I figured it was time to go. We went back to my place to get her car, and by the time we reached my house, she had passed out. I lugged her into the house, and sat her down on the couch and made her some coffee, which she didn't want. Finally I suggested she sleep in my bed while I slept on the couch, because she was in no shape to drive.

"I lay down on the couch, and about an hour later she was on top of me and all over me. I thought she was really attractive, but I didn't want to have sex under these conditions—she was still pretty high. I told her that I thought we should cool it, and she got mad and insisted that I walk her to her car. By now, it was about 3:30 in the morning. The most I could do was convince her to have some coffee, and then we walked to the car. I thought she was sober enough to drive, but I had barely come home and gotten back into bed when my phone rang. She had only driven a few blocks when she got sick, and called me. Once again I got out of bed, went and got her, helped her find a place to park her car, and drove her home—about thirty minutes away."

Danny invited Amelia out to dinner, but when he got to her house she insisted that they stay home, and she would cook instead. Danny says, "She was a terrible cook; I swear she basted a leg of lamb with Hawaiian Punch. It was awful. She said she wanted to stay in because she wanted to watch some opera on television. I had planned a nice dinner at a good restaurant. I ended up on her couch eating funny-tasting overcooked meat, watching Pavarotti or some other guy, and I hate opera. She also had three cats that kept getting their tails in my food."

THE SMARTEST WOMAN KNOWS . . .
Men Like Women Who Are Sensitive to Their Interests, Their Plans, and Their Friends.

Jason and his friend Glen figure that in the last year, between the two of them, they have gone out with approximately twenty women. Neither of them has taken out any of these women more than a few times. They both say the same thing: if the woman does something during the first few dates that makes them think a potential relationship would be too much of a hassle, they write it off and don't ask her out again. Many men feel this way, and women often don't understand what they've done that's created the difficulty. This is particularly true for the first few dates, when everyone is jumping to conclusions. Once a man comes to view a woman's behavior as seriously problematic, it's almost impossible to change his mind.

———— ❧ ————

The Smartest Woman Knows Certain Kinds of Behavior Are Neither Endearing nor Smart.

Some examples:

• He invites you to come with him to an Earth Day demonstration. His plan is to spend an afternoon walking around and sitting on the grass. You like nature, but not so much that you want to walk around in it. You show up in heels, and after what you think is an appropriate amount of time, you suggest going to a restaurant for lunch. After all, the idea was that you were going to be together. Right?

• He asks you to meet him at his *favorite* funky little coffee shop. When you get there, the first words out of your mouth are "I haven't eaten all day. Isn't there someplace we can go to get a real meal?"

• You both make plans to go to the beach. You arrive without a bathing suit, a towel, or sunblock.

• He asks you to go to a ball game, which means you have to take public transportation. You meet him on a street corner. You're wearing your great-grandmother's diamond ring, valued at over $10,000, and all you can talk about is whether or not you will be safe. He feels as though he can't leave your side even to get a hot dog or go to the bathroom, for fear of a mugging.

• You both agree to meet for a seven o'clock movie. You show up at seven twenty-five.

• He invites you to a party to meet some of his close friends for the first time. You get into a heavy, serious argument with his friend Frank because Frank bought his dog from a breeder instead of going to an animal shelter.

• He invites you to an expensive and wonderful restaurant because he's in the mood to celebrate life. He gets there first, and waits for you to arrive to help him choose the wine. You sit down saying you just started a new diet. All you'll have is some tea, and maybe some romaine—hold the dressing.

THE SMARTEST WOMAN KNOWS . . .

Men Like Women Who Don't Audition for Wife on the First Date.

Amanda wants very much to be some man's wife. She thinks she would be terrific in that role. She thinks she's supportive, loving, giving, fun, sexy, smart, and she wants to share those qualities with a loving man and a family. As fabulous as Amanda is (and she is fabulous), unless she changes her dating tactics, she may never get a chance to utilize any of her fine qualities.

You see, from the very first moments of the very first date with a man, all of her energy is directed at proving what a wonderful wife she would be. Amanda doesn't realize how obvious her intentions are, and she also doesn't realize how uncomfortable these intentions can make a man feel.

Yes, it's great that Amanda wants to get married, but she's not going to get married on the first date. At least we hope, for her sake—and his—that she's not. So why does she keep trying to insert her marital agenda into every conversation? It's amazing how competent Amanda is at turning every topic around so she can bring attention to her fine wifely qualities. For example:

He says, "I love pasta."

⟨≈⟩

THE SMARTEST WOMAN KNOWS . . .

Sometimes Giving Less Gets You More than Giving More.

She says, "I make some of the greatest pasta dishes. You'll love them."

He says, "My cousin Tom's having problems with his wife."

She says, "Women shouldn't behave that way. I would never do that."

In a myriad of ways, subtle and not so subtle, Amanda is always working to get the message across that she would be a terrific life partner. The Smartest Woman knows that the first date is her first chance to get to know someone and for him to get to know her. That's it. Trying to prove your "wifeliness" on the first date turns the date into an audition. And that's a very bad way to start.

———⟨≈⟩———

When she's with a new man, the Smartest Woman . . .

. . . doesn't coo every time she passes a cute baby.

. . . doesn't spend the entire evening talking about commitment.

. . . doesn't wax poetic about how much she loves children.

. . . doesn't dress, talk, sing, or dance like Mary Poppins.

. . . doesn't use her napkin to wipe smudges off *his* face.

. . . doesn't spend the entire evening talking about all her married friends in suburbia.

. . . doesn't talk about visiting her friends in sub-urbia *together*.

. . . doesn't offer to sew the loose button on his shirt.

. . . doesn't offer to press his clothing.

. . . doesn't try to get the food stain out of his tie with club soda.

. . . doesn't cook a gourmet dinner.

. . . doesn't offer to clean his apartment.

The Smartest Woman Knows that Women Who Audition for Wife on the First Date Rarely Get the Role.

THE SMARTEST WOMAN KNOWS . . .

Too Many Guys, Even Good Guys, Don't Appreciate Women Who Are Ready to Hand Themselves Over, No Questions Asked.

James, Kevin, and Michael are sitting around having a conversation about a woman Kevin has recently started dating. Let's listen to what they say:

James: So, what's happening between you and Cheryl? I saw you at the party last night, and she seemed to be really into you.

Kevin: Yeah, and it has me worried. I'm not sure where I want this relationship to end up. We don't know each other well enough, and to be honest, I don't know whether we have the same interests. Don't get me wrong, I really like being with her, but I don't want to disappoint her.

James: What are you going to do?

Kevin: I've been thinking about it. I guess I'll try to see her less often.

Michael: I wish I had that problem with Beth. I know she loves me, but man, is she putting me through the wringer.

THE SMARTEST WOMAN KNOWS . . .
Men Wonder About Women Who Get Too Interested Too Soon.

Cheryl has a problem that needs discussing here because it's a problem that she shares with many women. When Cheryl thinks someone likes her, she responds very quickly—*too quickly, in fact*. Sometimes she responds even if she isn't sure how much she likes the guy. It's almost as if there is some primal out-of-control hormonal timer that goes off automatically. This timer is so loud that it overwhelms many of her more self-protective impulses.

For example, when Cheryl met Kevin, a tall, very attractive salesman, at a party, she saw him flirting with another woman across a crowded room. Her immediate reaction was "I know the type, and I don't need it." But then Kevin came across the room to talk to her. At first, she held on to those initial feelings of mistrust. This made her appear distant, and Kevin had to work to get her attention. As he continued talking, however, and asked her out, she couldn't help responding.

By the end of the first date, she went from ice-cold to toasty warm. As far as she was concerned, he liked her, she liked him, and she was ready to move forward into another stage of the relationship. The problem is that Cheryl's first instincts were right: Kevin is a very difficult guy, and like many other guys—difficult and otherwise—he places more value on women when he has to work to hold their interest.

Perhaps if Cheryl had waited a little longer before she gave Kevin her unconditional acceptance and approval, he might have grown to care for her so much that her value would come from her place in his life. But she didn't. And now she has a problem.

Here's a rule:

THE SMARTEST WOMAN KNOWS . . .
Too Much Intensity Too Soon Is Too Much for Most Men to Handle.

Always remember that until the relationship has some mileage, the two of you are still finding out about each other. As much as you wish it were different, as much as you might like to immediately break down all the walls and be totally known to this man, it doesn't work that way. You're not an established couple, and you need to act in a way that reflects this fact. This doesn't mean that you want to treat him like a creep, but you can't move into his life overnight, and you shouldn't start helping him pack a U-Haul too quickly, either—even if he asks you to.

In the beginning, timing is everything. Even the most well-intentioned gesture, if it arrives prematurely, is grounds for suspicion. For many men, too much caring too soon feels like neediness, and it seems questionable. This is not about right versus wrong. It's about the right time versus the wrong time. It's about an appropriate response versus an inappropriate response. It's about going slow even when you've been invited to move fast. This is a difficult lesson for many women to learn, and with good reason, because women traditionally have been conditioned to do just the opposite.

THE SMARTEST WOMAN KNOWS . . .

• The More You Want to Race Forward, the More You Need to *Slow Down.*

———⟨⟩———

• You Have Nothing to Lose and Everything to Gain by Slowing Down.

———⟨⟩———

• The More He Tries to Accelerate the Relationship, the More *You* Need to *Slow It Down.*

The Smartest Woman Has the Strength, the Clarity, and the Confidence to Sit Back and Let the Beginning of the Relationship Evolve Slowly—As It Should.

THE SMARTEST WOMAN KNOWS . . .
Men Like Women Who Don't Scare Them to Death.

While many men are capable of being loving, supportive partners and good fathers, in their own fantasies men are more likely to see themselves as independent, rugged individualists who are in charge of their own destiny. The operative issue here is *control*. While many men ultimately make wonderful partners, few men "partner up" all that easily. Fear of losing control of the pacing and development of the relationship makes many men hit the panic button the moment it feels like too much is happening too soon. This is sometimes even true when it is the man who has pushed for greater intimacy and connectedness.

At some point in every relationship, the typical man will become extremely concerned about "going slowly," "holding back," "being careful," "not letting it go too far," and making sure his behavior isn't being "misinterpreted." That many men scare easily is just a fact of life. Women hate to be told this, and they don't always believe it anyway. While it's not your job to protect all these "sensitive" male psyches, you'd better be aware of what you're dealing with, because with some men the slightest sense of pressure terrifies them.

Today many men are wrestling with traditional roles versus progressive roles. Unlike women, there are very few men who are hoping to be swept off their feet and into a world of intense responsibility, diapers, mothers-in-law, large mortgage payments, and future college tuitions. This is not to say that they don't want these things eventually. But *eventually* means eventually. All of these things must slowly unfold. Slowly.

THE SMARTEST WOMAN KNOWS . . .
Anything That Feels Like "Too Much Too Soon" Is Going to Make a Man Feel that He Doesn't Have Control of His Own Destiny.

THE SMARTEST WOMAN KNOWS . . .

For Many Men, Too Sexual Too Soon Is Too Much.

Joseph and Miranda met at a party last week, and now they are sitting in a restaurant drinking espresso and sharing a sinfully rich double chocolate brownie with vanilla ice cream. Joseph's experience with women has taught him that for many women, chocolate is a major turn-on, and Joseph wants to turn Miranda on. Just watching Miranda digging into that brownie is a sensually exciting experience.

Wait a minute! *What is Miranda doing?* She's making major eye contact with Joseph. Look, she's cutting into the brownie with her spoon, adding some ice cream, and she's feeding it to Joseph. Now she's putting the spoon back into her mouth. She's licking it. She certainly seems turned on. Is this an invitation? For tonight? He definitely plans to find out. Isn't this what Joseph wanted? So why does he feel so uncomfortable? Why is he beginning to feel as though he would rather go home and watch CNN?

When it comes to women, Joseph thinks he has fairly typical responses. When he meets a new woman he likes, his thoughts immediately jump in one of two directions—sex or marriage. In his head, more often than not, he finds himself leaping forward to how this new woman will be in bed, and as a life partner. But while he is always thinking ahead, he is also always wary of a woman who appears to be doing the same thing. To put it bluntly, it scares him.

Women typically don't think of Joseph as the kind of man who scares easily. He seems confident and sure of himself. He seems worldly and smart. He seems savvy and knowledgeable about women. He even surfs and scuba dives. However, the fact remains that Joseph scares easily—and so do most men.

If, for example, Joseph has a date who responds to him as if she's known him for weeks, when she's known him for only a few hours, he wonders what's wrong with her, and it scares him. If she's known him for only a few weeks, and she's already acting like a long-term partner, a best friend, or a wife—long before he thinks these possibilities should have crossed her mind—*it scares him.*

When Joseph meets a woman, he needs time to let her into his world, and he wants her to take time to let him into hers. Inappropriate intimacy or inappropriate sexuality—*no matter how much he may seem to be inviting it*—makes him feel that the woman isn't relating to Joseph as Joseph. It makes him feel that the woman doesn't see him, doesn't hear him, doesn't understand him, and doesn't really have any true interest in doing so. It's as though she has her own internal agenda that kicks into operation on its own. In his head, he thinks that it can't possibly be in response to him, because she doesn't know him well enough. More often than not, on some subtle level, when a woman responds to him too intensely, too soon, he interprets it as some form of neediness or desperation. *That scares him even more!* She may think she's flattering him. But what's really happening is that she is terrifying him.

Why is Joseph so scared? Miranda is just being sexual. Doesn't he want a sexual woman? Yes, Joseph wants a sexual woman, but he doesn't feel as though Miranda is just being sexual. He feels she is also being controlling. Miranda seems to be trying to control the sexual agenda, and that makes him wonder whether there will be other agendas she will try to control. Joseph is beginning to feel as though he doesn't have choices. He's beginning to feel that something is being demanded of him. He's beginning to feel that she is orchestrating the seduction and she's playing the music too loud.

THE SMARTEST WOMAN KNOWS . . .
Men Don't Like Sexual Pressure Any More than Women Do.

The Smartest Woman Knows that a Man Appreciates a Woman Who Says He's a "Nice Guy" and Doesn't Mean It as an Insult.

THE SMARTEST WOMAN KNOWS . . .
Men Like Women Who Aren't Always Involved with Bad Boys.

A couple of years ago, Chris met a woman named Kayla at a club. They danced together a few times, and he drove her home. When he got her home, he discovered that she had a small child. Chris asked Kayla for her phone number and offered to drive home her mother, who had been baby-sitting. Chris called Kayla the following week, and even though she was very friendly on the phone, she put off seeing him. Finally she told him that she was still involved in a relationship with a man who kept being unfaithful. According to Kayla, she had gone to the club in an attempt to get even, but she couldn't follow through. Kayla told Chris that she really liked him, and she asked if *she* could call, if her situation changed.

About a year later, Chris ran into Kayla at a beach. She was with her son. She seemed very upset, and when they talked she told Chris that she and her boyfriend had recently broken up—she thought for the last time. Chris and Kayla spent that afternoon together, and Chris made a special effort to get along with her son, who seemed like a good little kid who needed some attention from a man.

Once again, Chris called Kayla. Once again, Kayla seemed friendly. And once again, Kayla put off seeing him. Chris says he has met many women like Kayla. They are sweet, sincere, kind, sensitive, and loving. But their hearts are tied up with some creep who is giving them grief. If you go out on a date with one of them, by the end of the evening she'll be telling you stories about how this creep ruined her birthday, ruined her vacation, and ruined her life. Chris says that life experience has taught him that these women are so busy trying to be good to some jerk that they don't have any room for a guy who wants to build a mutual relationship. What Chris says he finds particularly galling is the way these women "take care" of their bad boys. He says he finds it amazing the way some women can turn into emotional nursemaids for creepy guys who are walking all over them.

THE SMARTEST WOMAN KNOWS . . .

There's a Limited Supply of Decent, Loving Men Out There. If One Passes Your Way, Stop for a Minute and Pay Attention.

The Smartest Woman Knows When a Man Is Pushing All Her Buttons, and She Doesn't Let It Push Her to the Edge.

When Amy and Benjamin started dating, Amy was sure it was going to be a very meaningful relationship, but lately Benjamin has started to do and say things that make Amy anxious. Amy hasn't realized it yet, but Benjamin has a style of interacting with women that tends to make them insecure. Within the first few dates, he gives just enough to make a woman feel he can give a great deal, and then he typically withdraws. It's a very subtle kind of behavior that has the capacity to push a woman's buttons and turn her into the pursuer. Right now Amy's buttons are pushed. She's trying to get Benjamin to give what she thinks he's capable of giving.

What Amy needs to know is that Benjamin can't give that much. And his style, which throws the responsibility for the relationship at the woman, obscures his own shortcomings. Benjamin, for example, is rarely 100 percent faithful, but the way he does this makes a woman feel she can prove herself more worthy than other women. Instead of understanding that Benjamin has a problem, Amy worries about how to show him that she is all he would ever need in a woman. Amy is doing something that many women have done with many, many men like Benjamin. He's turned the tables so that she's barely paying attention to whether he's worth all this attention. Instead of proving her worthiness, she needs to take a much harder look at Benjamin.

The Smartest Woman Is Never So Concerned About the Impression She's Making that She Fails to Notice the Other Person's Potentially Fatal Flaw.

THE SMARTEST WOMAN KNOWS . . .
Neediness Will Often Turn a Good Guy Off, and a Bad Guy On.

We've got to talk about this. Divers know that when they are swimming in shark-infested waters, the slightest drop of blood is enough to attract a shark's attention. To a shark, blood signals that a creature is wounded and vulnerable. That combo spells lunch. Sometimes it seems as though the same thing is true in relationships. Too many women have discovered the hard way that when they are at their neediest, they are most likely to attract a shark.

THE SMARTEST WOMAN . . .
• Doesn't Make Herself Available to the World when She Needs to Be Taking Care of Herself.
• Doesn't Let Her Pain Be a Beacon for Every Pirate Ship on the High Seas.
• Doesn't Talk to Sharks when She's Feeling like a Guppie.

The Smartest Woman Knows the Difference Between . . .

- The Man Who's on the Ball and the Man Who's on the Brink.
- The Man Who Likes Women and the Man Who Takes Advantage of Women.
- The Man Who Wants Her in His Life and the Man Who Wants Her for the Night.
- The Man Who Plays Hockey and the Man Who Treats Her like a Puck.

THE SMARTEST WOMAN KNOWS . . .

- Your Family Doesn't Have to Look like the Munsters to Seem Peculiar.
- Your Mom Doesn't Have to Look like Morticia Addams to Seem Frightening.
- Your Dad Doesn't Have to Look like Superman to Seem Larger than Life.

We all have our family stories. Funny ones. Sad ones. Silly ones. Crazy ones. And scary ones. Sometimes in an effort to push for a closer connection, a woman can bury a new guy in family material. In other words, *stories* about your mom and dad that only present one side of their personalities can make them appear weird and off-putting. Too many stories about your family, and it can appear that your connections are so intense that there is no room for another person—specifically the man across the table.

Yes, your family connections are important, and in time all these stories about them can be shared. But not at the beginning of a new relationship, when *he* doesn't know *you* well enough to see you as an individual separate from the other individuals who comprise your family. Men often jump to the conclusion that their values are your values, their prejudices are your prejudices, their shortcomings are your shortcomings, and their likes and dislikes are your likes and dislikes.

Even things that you consider wonderful can seem

scary and intimidating to someone who doesn't know you or your nearest and dearest. Here's a good example:

For their first date, Andy and Janet went to a concert, and they had a terrific time. They discovered that they both liked the same music, they both laughed at the same jokes, and they both worked with computers. So they had a lot to talk about. Now, on their second date, they are having dinner in a restaurant. They have been talking about themselves, and by the time dessert arrives, Andy is wondering whether there will be a third date. What did Janet say or do? Well, let's listen in:

> *Janet:* My mom is so happy with my dad. I just hope I can be as happy someday. I think the main reason is that my dad is so romantic. He's always surprising my mother with presents. Last year he came home with an emerald-and-gold bracelet hidden in a bag of chocolate chip cookies. Another time he brought a fur coat home, hid it in a garbage bag, and then told my mom that it was full of old shirts he wanted her to throw in the washing machine. She was so surprised!

Romantic? For some, perhaps. But the word that is coming to Andy's mind is *expensive*! Janet's story about her parents is making him think that her expectations are out of his financial league. He is also fearing that he and Janet may have very different ideas about what it means to be romantic. For Andy, being romantic means a quiet walk on the beach at sunset, an unexpected love note or a small bouquet of fresh flowers. Not exactly gems and furs.

The sad part of this story is that Janet would be thrilled by any of Andy's romantic notions. And she doesn't really expect or need expensive gifts. If Andy knew Janet better, her family story might be easier to appreciate. Yet, at this early stage, it is misleading and off-putting.

THE SMARTEST WOMAN KNOWS . . .
Like Horror Stories, Family Stories Are Fun Around the Campfire, but They Can Be Off-putting When You're Out on a Date With Someone You Barely Know.

THE SMARTEST WOMAN KNOWS . . .

Men Like Women Who *Don't* Become Obsessed with Them.

In a Dating Situation, the Smartest Woman
Knows . . .

When a Woman Tries Too Hard, Some Men
Get Confused.

———⊙———

When a Woman Tries Too Hard, Some Men
Get Scared.

———⊙———

When a Woman Tries Too Hard, Some Men
Get Greedy.

———⊙———

When a Woman Tries Too Hard, Some Men
Get Spoiled.

———⊙———

When a Woman Tries Too Hard, Some Men
Get Going.

THE SMARTEST WOMAN KNOWS . . .
If You're Trying to Sell Yourself, You're Selling Yourself Short.

Erica never tries to sell herself on the first date, or on the second. But when she starts to like a man, something happens. She loses her confidence, she loses her center, and she loses her head. Instead of sitting back and allowing time to take its course, she becomes so proactive that it throws the dynamic of the relationship totally out of kilter. Because she's insecure, she starts trying to prove how nice she is, how smart she is, how talented she is, how desirable she is, and how irreplaceable she is.

Her insecurity, for example, sometimes makes her look for excuses to contact him. Even more distressing, her anxiety takes over much of her life, and she begins to spend too much time thinking about this man. When she does this, her activity seems to develop a life of its own. She can't restrain herself. Cards, notes, little presents, phone calls. If the man she likes catches a cold, she sends care packages and vitamin C; if he's working late at the office, she sends brownies and espresso; if he's taking a trip to the Caribbean, she sends sunblock. She doesn't want him to forget her, and she wants to convey that she likes him.

This kind of behavior can make the most desirable woman in the world appear needy and desperate. And that, in turn, can make the nicest guy in the world question her role in his life. After all, he ponders, what's wrong with her that she thinks so much of me? Is this a variation on the old Groucho Marx line, "I don't want to join any club that would have me as a member"? Probably. Is it human nature? Absolutely. The fact is, few of us are so saintly that we don't underestimate and undervalue people who are trying too hard to make us like them.

THE SMARTEST WOMAN KNOWS . . .

Excessive consideration, note sending, and gift giving is appropriate in a long-term relationship or marriage, particularly when you're trying to spice up the romance. Within the context of a new or potential relationship, it can easily be interpreted that you're trying to prove yourself.

THE SMARTEST WOMAN NEVER . . .
- Treats Any Date as Though It's Her Last.
- Treats Any Relationship as Though It's Her Life.

Heidi has always had serious abandonment issues, and she's very aware of them. For most of her twenties, whenever she met a guy she thought was interesting, the same thing would happen: they would go out, and then she would go home and worry about whether or not he was going to call. It was amazing! Within twenty-four hours, some man she barely knew was able to take over her dreams, her thoughts, and her feelings. Within twenty-four hours, a stranger would become the most meaningful issue in her life. Was this love? We don't think so.

Even Heidi saw the silliness in giving so much power to a stranger, and with a great deal of effort she was able to overcome her one-date madness. But overcoming her abandonment response to more important relationships was a little bit more serious. You see, if Heidi became involved with a man, all of her abandonment issues would surface within a very short time.

For example, let's take a quick look at Heidi's relationship with Brandon. Whenever Heidi was with Brandon, she felt an overwhelming need to try to cement the relationship permanently, and she wanted constant assurance that he cared. It was almost a craving. Brandon would tell Heidi that he loved her, and within an hour she would start worrying whether he *still* loved her. Whenever he left her, whether he was going to his apartment, his job, or around the corner to the grocery store, she would become concerned that he wasn't going to return. If he phoned her in the morning, by the afternoon she was feeling desperate and scared.

As you might imagine, Heidi's abandonment issues were the result of incidents that happened when she was a child. These early traumas were then compounded by a number of painful experiences in her first relationships as an adult. Eventually Heidi became so sensitized to the prospect of abandonment that her anxieties began to control her life. Reasonable men would sense Heidi's anxieties very quickly and would experience her as needy and emotionally burdensome.

Psychology teaches us that relationship development is a necessary process of connection, disconnection, and reconnection. You're together, and then you move away. You come *back* together and then you move away again. And then you repeat the process. As uncomfortable as this is for many of us, there is no way around it—not if you want a relationship that is healthy.

In our fantasies, sometimes we see ourselves always with the one we love. Or at least separating when *we* want to separate. But that's not how relationships work. No matter how much someone loves you, no matter how good a couple the two of you make, you each need time alone. You each have jobs, you each have friends, you each have individual noncouple needs, and you each need to go to sleep at night. All of these things are going to require some separation. And this is something you're going to have to get used to.

These separations are particularly traumatic for individuals who struggle with abandonment issues from childhood, but they also give them a unique opportunity to rework some of those early struggles in a healthier way. If you can't handle being apart from the one you love—if, every time he is gone for more than an hour, you imagine he's either dead or in someone else's bedroom—then you need to do some serious work. Awareness is your first goal in dealing with this problem. Codependency groups and other twelve-step programs are excellent and inexpensive ways to help you become aware of the ways in which abandonment issues could be controlling your life.

A Smart Woman Doesn't Let Her Abandonment Ghosts Spook a Potential Partner.

The Smartest Woman Knows that Nothing Short of Krazy Glue Can Keep Two People Together Every Single Moment.

THE SMARTEST WOMAN . . .

- Never Feels Dead When the Line Goes Dead.
- Never Thinks She's Lost the Connection Every Time She Hangs Up the Phone.
- Never Thinks Hanging On to the Phone Is Going to Help Her Hang On to Him.

Lucas says that he was looking forward to going out with Holly. He had met her at a party, and she seemed attractive and nice. When he called her on the phone to set up the date, she seemed interesting and interested. But for Lucas, it was all downhill after that, and he says it was Holly's phone behavior that turned him off.

Lucas and Holly talked on the phone on Tuesday night, and they agreed to meet at a coffeehouse on Thursday for cappuccino and dessert. Wednesday, Holly called Lucas to confirm the date. To Lucas this seemed unnecessary because they had just talked. Lucas was working on his computer when she called, and he didn't have time to talk. His distracted tone seemed to make Holly anxious, and instead of getting off the phone, she kept asking him questions: "What are you doing?" "How do you get on the Internet?" "How long have you had the computer?" "Do you like it?"

When Lucas first met Holly, she had seemed very desirable, but suddenly she began to appear overly needy and dependent. When they met for coffee, once again Holly looked attractive and charming. When they said good night, Lucas was thinking that he would let it sit for a few days, then he would probably call her and ask her to go with him to a concert the following week. But by the time Lucas walked into his apartment, his phone was ringing. It was Holly, calling from her car phone to tell him what a nice time she had.

This scared him! Scenes from *Fatal Attraction* began to race across his brain. All he could think of were dead bunnies and a nervous-looking Michael Douglas. He says that it made him think: "This woman doesn't even know who I am. Why is she acting as though we are having a passionate romance?" Lucas felt as though he wasn't being allowed to come up for air, and he decided that the best thing he could do was not go out with Holly again.

Yes, some women would say that Lucas was being totally wimpy. But Lucas is basically a nice guy. He wants a normal relationship with a normal woman. To him, excessive neediness seems frightening. It doesn't fit his image of what he wants for his future. Yes, Lucas was attracted to Holly, but he made a "practical" decision based on limited information. He wants to get out before it gets more complicated, and that's what he is afraid will happen if he sees Holly again.

The Smartest Woman Doesn't Need to Check Her Watch to Know When It's Time to Say Goodbye.

THE SMARTEST WOMAN KNOWS . . .
Men Like Women Who Know How to Let Go and Move On.

BUT THAT'S NOT WHY YOU SHOULD DO IT!!! When a relationship isn't happening, when a relationship isn't working out, when a relationship isn't fulfilling, the Smartest Woman lets go and moves on. _But she does it for herself, not for any man._

Dealing with rejection and dealing with disappointment are two of the toughest lessons any of us has to learn. Yet these lessons seem to go hand in hand with dating and romance. The hard truth is that not all dates turn into relationships, not all relationships turn into marriages, and not all marriages last. These are facts of life. Here's another fact of life: When a relationship doesn't become what you want it to be, you should be grateful. Almost inevitably, you will come to see that you and this other person were not right for each other.

Think back to your great-grandmother's life. Often, the only man she kissed was the one she would marry. Her marriage might even have been arranged. If _her_ parents were discerning, she got lucky. If not, she was stuck.

Today none of us has to be stuck in relationships that don't work out. So if your relationship isn't working out, if some blind date isn't calling to ask you out for a second date, if some man you just met "lost" your phone number, if the man in your life is being controlling, selfish, unfaithful, uncaring, ungiving, hostile, or just plain rejecting, you're a lucky woman! You have a reprieve! You are not going to have to spend the rest of your life with a man who doesn't appreciate your wonderful qualities, your lovely essence, your beautiful spirit, or your unique personality.

Of course, you have to mourn the loss of a person you cared about. Of course, you can't move on until you've processed the experience. But don't get maudlin, don't get obsessed, and don't get stuck. You're the lucky one: you have a chance to start over and a chance to start smarter.

The Smartest Woman Treats Every Breakup as *His* Loss.

The Smartest Woman Knows the Difference Between Myth and Fact.

Myth: It was a love that was meant to be.

Fact: It was hormones. We are all prisoners of our own chemistry from time to time. But even your chemistry professor will tell you that there's a lot more to life than molecules.

Myth: It was a love that was meant to be.

Fact: It was a trick. He knew what you wanted and let you think he could deliver it. He can't. Time to move on.

Myth: It was a love that was meant to be.

Fact: It was a mistake. We all make mistakes. It's part of being human. But don't turn an honest mistake into a ten-year ordeal just because you can't admit that you erred.

Myth: It was a love that was meant to be.

Fact: It was the moon. When the setting was perfect, he seemed perfect. But many moons have passed, and now you'd be better off running with the wolves.

THE SMARTEST WOMAN KNOWS . . .

It's Never Smart to Give Away All Your Power.
It's Never Smart to Usurp All His Power, Either.

THE SMARTEST WOMAN KNOWS . . .

High-Maintenance Women Are like High-Maintenance Cars . . . Fun to Look At, but Not Very Practical.

John says that when he first starts dating someone, he wants to make sure that this woman will not turn into a "high-maintenance" girlfriend. This is something he and his friends discuss often. They all want to make sure that the women they end up with will not make unreasonable demands or have unreasonable expectations. Here's how John explains it: "It's really just basic economics. You know, supply and demand. And I can't afford to be with a woman who demands more than I can supply. The bottom line is that some women are too much work."

John and his friends believe there are two separate categories of high-maintenance women:

1. *Women who cost too much financially*

Some women are focused on material stuff. Take them out for a few times and you have to apply for a grant. John and his friends say they check out, in the following ways, whether or not they can afford a woman.

• Does she automatically gravitate toward expensive items? What does she look at in store windows, what does she talk about wanting, and what does she order in restaurants?

- Does she seem to reject simple pleasures (a ball game, a hot dog) in favor of more lavish entertainment (expensive theater or concert tickets, a meal at a posh restaurant)?
- What impresses her? Big houses, big cars, big expense accounts?
- Is she dressed so expensively that she looks like a tax shelter?

2. *Women who cost too much emotionally*

Some women have excessive emotional demands. John and his friends feel they are like little kids who want their hands held. Here's what they are on the lookout for:

- Does she have a million and one crises and traumas that need attending?
- Does she insist upon being the center of attention?
- Does she make scenes and create problems?
- Does she alienate people?
- Does she make unreasonable demands?
- Does she have unreasonable expectations?
- Does she personalize everything?
- Does she seem as fragile as glass?
- Does she always need someone to defend her?

The Smartest Woman Knows the Difference Between . . .

- Looking Enticing and Looking Extravagant.
- Looking Attractive and Looking Unafford-able.
- Looking Beautiful and Looking Burden-some.
- Being Interesting and Being Exhausting.
- Being Cute and Being Combative.
- Being Magnetic and Being Manipulative.

The Smartest Woman Knows that a Man Wants to Be with a Woman Who . . .

- Values His Character More than His Cash Flow.
- Wants His Company More than She Wants His Car.
- Likes His Personality More than She Likes His Portfolio.
- Appreciates His Humor More than She Appreciates His House.

THE SMARTEST WOMAN KNOWS . . .
Men Like Women Who Understand the Concept of 50-50.

Russell, 34, says that he's had relationships that he would define as 70-30. He's given 70 percent; she's given 30 percent. He hated that. He also said he's had relationships that he would call 30-70. He's given 30 percent; she's given 70 percent. According to him, he hated that feeling even more. What he would like is a relationship that is truly 50-50. A relationship where there is a balance of give-and-take, a balance of caring and being cared for, helping and being helped, loving and being loved.

Russell says that many of the women he meets don't have a sense of balance, and by that he doesn't mean they are emotionally disturbed. What he means is they are either doing and giving so much that he feels overwhelmed, smothered, and guilty, or doing and giving so little that he feels resentful and used. Some women have been conditioned to do all of the giving. Others are more than ready to sit back and feel totally taken care of. But neither one of these styles is balanced, and in the long run, neither one works.

THE SMARTEST WOMAN KNOWS . . .

Walking Hand in Hand Through a Relationship Means Walking a Fine Line Between Giving Too Much and Giving Too Little.

THE SMARTEST WOMAN KNOWS . . .
Men Like Women Who Carry Their Own Baggage.

Bob says he has gone out with quite a few women in the last few years, and something always goes wrong, which makes him feel he doesn't want to pursue the relationship any further. The deal breaker almost always revolves around the following issue: No matter how much the woman talks about equal rights, she still wants to be treated as though she's not truly accountable for anything, let alone 50 percent of the partnership. For example, he's expected to assume responsibility for the tab, except when she *feels* like contributing.

Bob says something happened recently with an old girlfriend that really gave him pause. When they were going out, she borrowed a small television set to take to work. The relationship was never that serious for either one of them, and eventually they stopped seeing each other. They had a couple of pleasant phone conversations, so there was no animosity. Then, a week ago, Bob's television broke, and he remembered the one he had loaned her. So he called. She was really annoyed. As far as she was concerned, the relationship was over, the contact with him was over, and the TV was hers to keep.

What bothered Bob was that she refused to be accountable. She had borrowed something, and it was appropriate to return it. But instead of seeing this as an exchange between two mature adults, Bob's ex-girl-friend saw the television as a casualty of the relation-ship. To him this was further proof that many women today want it both ways. They want equality, but they also want to be taken care of and coddled.

THE SMARTEST WOMAN KNOWS . . .
Men Have Trouble Kissing a Woman Who Is Always Talking Out of Both Sides of Her Mouth.

Myth: Men Like Women Who Give Them a Hard Time.

Fact: Some Men Like Women Who Give Them a Hard Time. And These Men Are Not Necessarily the Healthiest Bunch of Men.

Women often ask why so many men seem to pay so much more attention to women who keep them guessing and slightly off balance. Is that really what they prefer? Well, the truth is that over the long haul, men don't prefer women who give them a hard time. However, at the beginning of a relationship, men do seem to maintain more interest in women who allow for some distance and some mystery.

Nonetheless, with some men, it's always a no-win situation. If you're angry, annoyed, difficult, moody, petulant, selfish, destructive, manipulative, dishonest, and self-absorbed, you can make real headway with one of these guys. Otherwise, men like this will never appreciate your value, and they will never appreciate how much you care.

THE SMARTEST WOMAN KNOWS . . .
If the Only Thing That Turns Him On Is Seeing You Turn Off, He Has a Real Problem. Don't Make It Yours!

The Smartest Woman Knows How Much She Can Give and How Much She Will Put Up With.

Whether she's in a relationship or out of a relationship, the Smartest Woman always has a bottom line. And she makes sure that the man she's with, or any man she goes out with, has a sense of that bottom line. We've all heard men say things like "Oh, sure I look at other women, but if I ever did anything more than look, my wife would be out the door." "I don't play golf on Sundays because my wife insists that we spend time as a family." "My girlfriend is very clear on this—she makes dinner for me, I make dinner for her. What's fair is fair."

These men are not henpecked. They are with women who are very, very clear about what they will and will not tolerate. This clarity is part of the reason why they have power in their relationships. Of course, some men will avoid women who can't be walked over, but these aren't the men you want in your life, anyway.

When the Smartest Woman is in a relationship, she expects to be honest, faithful, fair, and well-intentioned. She expects the same from the man in her life. She knows that if she doesn't get what she deserves, he's history, and she makes sure that he knows it.

The Smartest Woman Isn't Afraid to Let the Man She Loves Be a Little Bit Afraid of Her Power.

Stage Two
Getting Closer

Congratulations. You've met a guy you like. And he seems to like you. So what are you worried about? Shouldn't it get easier, not harder, once the ice has been broken and the attraction is clear?

Well, the truth is, it's more complicated than that. For one thing—let's face it—even the greatest man in the world is still going to be very different from you. After all, he's a guy, you're not. It's that gender thing. Of course, that's part of the fun. But there are also other differences that make the terrain challenging and difficult.

This is where the hard part ends and the harder part begins. Beginnings may be scary, but getting closer is truly terrifying. Commitment anxieties begin to emerge. The relationship is getting real, and you and your partner may be starting to have small disagreements and conflicts. You have issues to resolve with each other. And, as you get closer, you each may find that you have your own personal issues to resolve.

When a couple barely knows one another, each partner can hide a great deal from the other. But when you start to get closer, vulnerabilities appear, and one or both of you may start to get nervous. When two people first start dating, the risks are relatively small. But if those same two people actually begin to get closer, and begin to construct a real relationship, the risks are enormous. Fasten your seat belts. Getting closer means being able to endure extraordinary vulnerability, periods of total anxiety, and a grab bag of other emotions too numerous to list. This is tough stuff.

THE SMARTEST WOMAN KNOWS . . .

Making an Intimate Connection with a Man Is Going to Stir Up Every Past Intimate Connection, Both Good and Bad, That You Have Ever Had with Any Other Human Being.

This is by no means limited to old beaus, ex-husbands, and hopeless crushes. We're talking about *every* connection since the day your scrunched-up little face emerged from the birth canal. Your mother. Your father. Your nanny, if you had one. Your grandmas and grandpas. Your aunts, your uncles. And don't forget those siblings, and their rivalries. Not to mention neighbors, teachers, and even preachers, if they were an important part of your life. The memories of all those intimate experiences live within each of us.

This is something our friend Candace is learning. She and Adam have been going out for about two months, and they're starting to see more of each other. They go out every weekend, they try to get together at least once in the middle of the week, they talk on the phone almost every day, and they're thinking of planning a vacation together. This week their relationship hit a crisis point.

Candace has already become accustomed to hearing from Adam every Friday morning to set up a plan for the weekend. On Thursday night, on an impulse, Adam drove to his parents' house in the suburbs to see his younger sister, who was home from college because she was having some problems. Adam stayed up talking with her until very late. When he woke up, it was such a beautiful morning that he decided not to go to work, and instead to spend some more time with his sister, who really needed support. He figured he would touch base with Candace later in the day.

Candace, in the meantime, had to leave her office for an all-day meeting, and she called Adam's office so he wouldn't miss her. Adam's receptionist said that he was out of town and wouldn't be back until Monday. Candace immediately jumped to all the wrong conclusions. This was based not just on what she was told, but also on her experiences with her ex-husband, who was very unreliable. When Candace and Adam finally got to talk on Friday evening, Candace was so upset she could barely speak. Adam didn't understand her problem, but he had a problem of his own.

When Adam's mother gets angry, she stops speaking. This is how she punishes family members. No amount of coaxing can make her speak until she's good and ready. It's a quality that drives Adam up the wall—so when Candace didn't talk, he jumped to his own conclusions. And he retaliated in his family style by withdrawing, thinking that Candace would get in touch with him when she calmed down. Candace, on the other hand, wanted warmth and understanding to help rebuild the trust she felt she had lost. Adam's response to her response only made her feel worse. Do you see how this works? Do you see how everything can get blown way out of proportion?

The Smartest Woman realizes that as she gets to know another person she's getting to see how his family interacts. It doesn't matter if that family is around the block, thousands of miles away, or resting peacefully at Forest Lawn. Styles of interaction that developed in our individual families are carried with us into every one of our adult relationships.

Spending time with a man means spending time with the remnants of his family system. There's good stuff, and there's always some negative stuff. And while you are getting to know his family through his behavior, he is also getting to know yours. Unless you've had a great deal of therapy, you are likely to interpret your partner's behavior the same way you interpret the behavior of your parents or siblings. You are likely to imagine your partner's needs as well as his reactions to specific occurrences as being similar to the needs and reactions of the people with whom you grew up. But this man is not a member of your family. He is not going to respond to you as your parents did. He is not going to react to you like your siblings did. And he is not your crazy uncle Phil. Your job is to hold on to this information and do everything you can to keep experiencing this man as the individual that he is.

THE SMARTEST WOMAN KNOWS . . .

Don't Turn Him Into Your Sibling, and Don't Turn On Him like a Sibling.

Don't Turn Him Into Your Father, and Don't Treat Him like a Father.

Don't Turn Him Into Your Mother, and Don't Fight with Him like He's Your Mother.

THE SMARTEST WOMAN KNOWS . . .

Men Appreciate a Woman Who Knows the Difference Between the Guy She's with Right Now and the Guy Who Stood Her Up in High School.

Let's talk for a minute about another reason why Candace is so quick to jump to the wrong conclusions. As an adult, Candace has had a string of disappointments in her human interactions. Her ex-boyfriend, her ex-husband, and her ex-roommate were all unreliable. They made promises they didn't keep, and they abused Candace's trust. Candace's history has given her good reason to assume the worst.

The very first second that Adam wasn't where she expected him to be, she assumed he would *never* be where she expected him to be. In fact, Candace doesn't know Adam well enough to be 100 percent certain that he is either trustworthy or untrustworthy. He may well turn out to be as big a creep as the last guy. However, she has to wait to get that information. Until then, she needs to be genuinely self-protective. She needs to get more facts before she turns over her heart. She needs to risk a little without risking a lot. The Smartest Woman knows that if you always assume the worst, you're not giving the relationship an honest chance.

The Smartest Woman Knows the Difference Between . . .

- Being Self-protective and Shooting Herself in the Foot.
- Being Cautious and Being Cowardly.
- An Isolated Incident and a Dedicated Lifestyle.

THE SMARTEST WOMAN KNOWS . . .

1 Woman + 1 Rigid Set of Expectations = 1 Guaranteed Disaster.

THE SMARTEST WOMAN KNOWS . . .
Men Like Women Who Don't Insist upon Formulas.

"After six months, he has to make a commitment." "If we go out more than three times, we have to establish a sexual relationship." "If we establish a sexual relationship, we have to have sex at least three times a week." "If he really loves me, he'll buy me a really nice present on Valentine's Day." "He's like most men; he won't be ready for marriage until he's earning six figures." "I won't marry him until he's earning at least fifty percent more than I am." "I expect a diamond on our first anniversary." "Once we get married, we should be able to buy our first house within the first year. Two at the latest." "I expect to get pregnant eighteen months after we get married."

Formulas may be very comforting, but they are not very realistic, and they're not helpful. Formulas inhibit spontaneity, and chances are that if you're looking at the formula, you'll be missing much that's happening in the relationship. Your relationship is unique, and it has to evolve on its own and in its own way.

THE SMARTEST WOMAN KNOWS . . .
Even if You're Dreaming About Forever, You

Have to Live One Day at a Time, Otherwise You're Not Living.

———— ◦∞◦ ————

The Only Thing You Can Truly Count On Is that There Is Very Little That You Can Count On.

———— ◦∞◦ ————

If You Need Formulas You Can Count On, Become a Mathematician.

The Smartest Woman Doesn't Talk About Where or How Her Ex Marked the Spot.

THE SMARTEST WOMAN KNOWS . . .
Men Like Women Who Reveal Their Sexual History on a Need-to-Know Basis.

Jessica feels so close to Charles that she thinks it's appropriate to share some of the details of her sexual history. She loves him, so she wants him to understand her and to know what was meaningful, what was painful, what was stupid, and what was fun. But when she starts to talk to him, the expression on his face (which he tries to hide) tells her that she'd better back off—and fast. Why? Why can't she talk to him honestly?

Let's face it. There are very few women who don't have a sexual history that predates their current partner. And it's understandable that a woman doesn't want to hide anything from the man she loves. Understandable. But not always smart. Sexual history, especially if it's a rich history, should be shared in the most gentle fashion and in the smallest of increments. Yes, some men handle this kind of information well. But many more don't. Talking about another man invites comparison and competition. No matter how confident the man, this stuff is hard to digest. Treat it like any substance that's hard to digest. Spoon-feed it, and only if necessary.

As liberated as any of us are, digesting the sexual past of someone you love is a challenge for every man and every woman. In truth, many men are really quite romantic, even if they don't appear that way. These men may be able to live with the fact that the woman they love has a sexual past in which they were not included. What they may have a harder time dealing with is that the present doesn't feel special.

It's hard to believe everything is special if you keep bringing a rogues' gallery of faces into the picture. They want to be able to believe that what the two of you are doing together has never been done before in the history of mankind, even if they know that isn't true. The more special your relationship feels, the harder it becomes to allow someone else's presence to intrude on your lovemaking. The Smartest Woman may have a lot of great stories about her old beaus, but even so, she never turns them into bedtime stories.

The Smartest Woman Never, Ever, Ever Says . . .
- Oh, That Reminds Me of Fred, only He Didn't Tickle.
- Ted Liked It That Way Too.
- I Never Missed with Ed.
- Ned Always Paid Attention when I Told *Him* What I Liked.

THE SMARTEST WOMAN KNOWS . . .

When It Comes to Sexual Intimacy, There Is Nothing Impressive About Name-dropping.

The Smartest Woman Knows that Extreme Sexual Jealousy Is a Serious Problem That Needs a Serious Solution.

Some men are frighteningly jealous, and we all have to recognize that. But if you're involved with a man like this, his behavior may be confusing. His passion for you may be so compelling that at first his over-the-top jealousy can seem flattering. Frequently such a man may appear obsessed with hearing all the details of your sexual past. He may say that only when he knows everything will he be able to "trust" you. We want to warn you that this kind of scenario is frequently a setup for disaster, and an extremely jealous man can easily become emotionally or physically abusive.

The Smartest Woman Knows that if You're Involved with an Intensely Jealous Man, You Need to Talk to a Professional Counselor or Therapist to Get the Advice You Need. This Is Never an Issue to Be Taken Lightly.

———— ∾⊗∾ ————

THE SMARTEST WOMAN KNOWS . . .
Men Like Women Who Understand the Concept of Private Space.

Boundaries. Boundaries. Boundaries. It's a buzzword for the nineties. But what's all the buzz about? Everyone tells you that it's important to have healthy boundaries, but no one tells you precisely what that means. To understand how boundaries work, think about how your family treats each other's space and each other's privacy. In life, each of us carves a little space around ourselves and puts up some kind of psychic wall or barrier. These walls represent our boundaries. Some people have very low walls with very large windows and doors. Others have very high walls with windows and doors that are very small and hard to locate. Some men and women open their doors and windows and share their space freely; others add extra bricks and supports the moment someone gets close.

In some families, nothing is too intimate, too private, too sacred. For these families, all doors are permanently open and boundaries are not clearly defined. Members of these families practically give daily reports on each other's stool samples. They call each other dozens of times a day, reporting every event, every hurt feeling, every detail of daily life, from what was eaten to what was expelled. "What are you feeling, what are you doing, what are you thinking? Tell me everything." There is a constant, ongoing engagement in each other's lives as well as their thoughts. Brother asks: "What's wrong with Sister?" He's told: "She got her period last night, and she's having terrible cramps. Go to the store and get her some tampons."

At the opposite end of the spectrum are families in which everything is hidden, everything is concealed, everything is secret, and all doors are closed. "What were Mom and Dad whispering about in the kitchen?" "Who knows!" "Why did Dad visit the doctor last week?" "Shhh! Don't ask! He's not telling!" Brother asks: "What's wrong with Sister?" He's told: "I don't know, and if she wants me to know, she'll tell me. Please close the door as you're leaving."

Of course, most families fall somewhere in the middle. But in each family there are usually areas where there are minimal boundaries and major boundaries. The Smith family, for example, is very private when it comes to emotional matters. Mr. and Mrs. Smith would never pry into their children's emotional lives. However, they are very intrusive when it comes to physical issues. Although John Smith, Jr., is thirty years old, his mother still calls to inquire what he had for dinner, but she never asks about his divorce. She considers that too private.

How you interact with another person as an adult,

and how he interacts with you, has much to do with the kinds of boundaries that existed in your family when you were growing up. You, for example, may have accepted your family's notion of boundaries without ever questioning them. Perhaps your partner, on the other hand, considered his family intrusive and upsetting. He may yearn for private space in ways that you can't understand. Or maybe it's the opposite. Perhaps your family is so private and formal with one another that when you hear friends complain about their intrusive mothers, you feel envious.

Whether you're doing the same thing, or purposely doing the opposite, almost inevitably your notion of appropriate boundaries is going to have everything to do with how your family behaved with one another. And there are boundary concerns with almost every issue that occurs between two people. Take affection, for example. Some people hug and kiss freely without giving it a second thought. Others consider their bodies private space, and only want to be hugged under certain circumstances and in certain ways. Money, food, sex, emotions. All of these create boundary issues. Can you touch each other's money, can you touch each other's food, can you touch each other's genitals, can you touch each other's private thoughts?

There are married couples who talk about divorce when all either of the partners really wants is a weekend alone. The boundaries that you establish in your relationship depend upon the ground rules that you both set up. All that matters is that you keep talking about them.

The Smartest Woman Knows the Difference Between . . .

* Wanting to Break Up and Wanting Time Alone.

* Wanting to Break Up and Wanting Your Own Space.

* Wanting to Break Up and Wanting Your Own Sandwich.

THE SMARTEST WOMAN KNOWS . . .
Men Like Women Who Don't Open Their Mail.

Ashley is feeling very jealous. And with some justi-fication. Her boyfriend, Paul, is seeing another woman. And it's not the first time, either. Right now Ashley is waiting for Paul to leave the room so she can do a quick check of his jacket for evidence. *Ashley, please stop what you're doing*.

Have you ever felt the way Ashley feels? So inse-cure in a relationship that you found yourself checking his shirts, his sheets, his appointment book, and his gar-bage can for the slightest shred of bad news? Clearly, like Ashley, you were having a problem with trust. Per-haps, like Ashley, your issues with trust were justified. However, this kind of behavior also indicates a problem with boundaries. Yes, everyone has felt the urge to snoop through her or his beloved's private stuff. This kind of boundary issue is understandable and human. However, it's never, ever, justifiable. If your trust is be-ing betrayed, and you can't handle or resolve the rela-tionship, the Smartest Woman tracks down a therapist or support group to help her do the kind of emotional investigating that is really called for.

THE SMARTEST WOMAN KNOWS . . .

His Stuff Is His Stuff, and You Don't Belong In It. And Your Stuff Is Your Stuff, and He Doesn't Belong In It.

THE SMARTEST WOMAN KNOWS . . .

If You're a Little Bit Jealous, a Man Can Feel Flattered. If You're Excessively Jealous, He May Think It's Time to Call the Witness Protection Program.

THE SMARTEST WOMAN KNOWS . . .

She Doesn't Have to Blow Up Balloons, Juggle Batons, Stand On Her Head, or Get Fido to Do Stupid Pet Tricks Every Time There's a Lull in the Conversation.

THE SMARTEST WOMAN KNOWS . . .
Men Like Women Who Aren't Afraid of Silence.

Bryan and Sara have had dinner, they've cleaned up after dinner, and they've made love. Bryan is feeling pretty good about Sara and the relationship. That's the thought in his head when he picks up a book that he's been planning to read for ages. He's happy that Sara is with him. He's happy that he feels comfortable enough to read while she's in the room.

Sara, on the other hand, watches Bryan pick up his book, and she goes into a mild panic. Is this normal, she wonders? Am I boring him? What can I do to be interesting? Why aren't we communicating? Why don't we have anything to talk about?

Sara is so nervous about silence that when conversation stops, she feels as though her heart has stopped. She'd do anything to get it going again. She honestly believes that she has to be lively, entertaining, engaging, and enthralling for hours at a time. She's always working, and she's never quiet.

The real problem here is that Sara feels abandoned in the silence. That's because Sara's feelings have a lot more to do with how she defines her role as a woman and her mixed-up expectations of how she thinks a relationship should evolve. In Sara's head, if a couple is happy together, they'll be talking all the time. About what, she's not sure. Because of these expectations, when there's silence, she gets scared that the relationship is dying, and she feels that she personally has to *do* something to keep it alive. That's quite a contrast from Bryan. To Bryan, the silence means a chance to relax and enjoy Sara's presence without actually having to do anything. That's all it means.

The Smartest Woman Knows the Difference Between a Healthy Silence and a Stony Silence.

The Smartest Woman Has the Courage to Draw a Line in the Sand Without Worrying About Spoiling Everyone's Day at the Beach.

THE SMARTEST WOMAN KNOWS . . .
Men Like Women They Can't Take Advantage Of.

Carmen is making Derek slightly nuts. The reason? She doesn't protect herself emotionally from the million and one demands that everyone makes on her. She never says *no*. And, yes, Derek knows that often his demands are also outrageous, and that she should say no to him as well.

Derek says that he was brought up in a household where everyone was taught to take care of themselves. That's what he expects Carmen to do. If he shows up at his mother's house and says "What's for dinner?" his mom answers, "Whatever you're cooking, and make enough for me because I'm hungry too." When Derek shows up at Carmen's apartment and asks what's for dinner, Carmen runs to the grocery store or the stove.

If Derek leaves his dirty socks on the bathroom floor at his mom's house, his mom hands them to him in a plastic bag for him to take home and wash. If he leaves his socks on Carmen's floor, she hands them back to him clean and folded.

It sounds as if Derek has it made. So why is he complaining? Because he doesn't like feeling guilty. He doesn't want to have to censor all of his knee-jerk sloppy guy behavior. That's too much work. Why can't Carmen learn to say *no* and fight back a little?

And there's another problem. It's not just Derek that Carmen can't say no to. Carmen rarely says no to anybody. Her phone rings off the hook with demands, emotional and otherwise, from her friends, her family, and her co-workers. If anyone is going to be working late, it's Carmen. If anyone is going to be answering a ringing phone at 3 A.M. because some crying person wants to talk about his or her romantic troubles, it's Carmen. Derek is not stupid. When he looks at Carmen he realizes that between her friends' demands, her work demands, and *his* demands, she's exhausted. He's worried that if they get married, all these people who make demands on her will end up making demands on him as well. He's also worried about how much time they will have together. Derek is happy that Carmen is such a good person, but enough already!

The Smartest Woman Doesn't Have to Answer the Phone Just Because It's Ringing.

The Smartest Woman Doesn't Have to Talk to Strangers Just Because They Talk to Her.

The Smartest Woman Doesn't Have to Answer a Question Just Because Somebody Asked It.

———◦∞◦———

The Smartest Woman Doesn't Have to Say Yes When She Wants to Say No.

———◦∞◦———

The Smartest Woman Never Gives Anything in Order to Get Something Back. The Smartest Woman Gives Because She Can and Because She Wants To.

THE SMARTEST WOMAN KNOWS . . .
Men Like Women Who Don't Keep Score.

Jeff complains that his girlfriend, Sharon, is perfect. She does everything. Then she complains about it, or holds it up to him. It has gotten to the point where Jeff is afraid to let her do anything for him because he can't stand her scorekeeping. He says, "Last night she made dinner, and I swear I didn't want to eat it. I know that next week, she'll point it out to me at least a dozen times how she made me dinner, and how I never do enough for her. I swear she only does things to get me to do things. It's always tit for tat, and it's like she's got some massive computer going all the time that keeps track of everything."

In an ongoing relationship, who can keep track of everything? Who changed the beds last week? Who did the laundry yesterday? Who shopped for dinner tonight? Who agreed to see a movie when he or she didn't want to? Who helped entertain whose parents? Who cooked chicken soup when the other one got sick? Who helped type whose term paper? Who did the driving? Who walked the dog? Who cleaned the bathtub? And how about the emotional stuff? Who is more supportive? Who is more caring? Who is more nurturing?

Often women find themselves giving more than they may want to in the hope of getting something in return. This is a human reaction. Unfortunately, it often doesn't work out that way.

THE SMARTEST WOMAN KNOWS . . .

If You Need to Do Something with Strings Attached, Go Fly a Kite.

The Smartest Woman Knows the Difference Between . . .

- Giving Someone a Gift and Giving Someone Guilt.
- Making Someone Happy and Making Someone Beholden.
- Giving Someone a Present and Giving Someone the Willies.

THE SMARTEST WOMAN KNOWS . . .

Two Hearts That Beat as One Is a Great Premise for a Sci-fi Movie, and a Horrible Premise for a Healthy Relationship.

THE SMARTEST WOMAN KNOWS . . .

Men Like Women Who Don't Think that Acting like a Couple Means Acting like the Two Halves of a Popsicle.

Jordan has just walked in the door, returning from an insanely difficult day at work. All he wants to do is turn on the news for fifteen minutes, get something to drink, and unwind. Tiffany is there at the door with hugs and kisses and a dozen questions about his day. How can he tell her that he just needs space and time alone and that it has nothing to do with his feelings about her?

Howard and Krista have just arrived at the Christmas party given by some of their friends. Howard sees some people he wants to talk to, but every time he tries to take a step in any direction, Krista is right at his heels, hanging on his arm. Howard loves Krista, but he hates this kind of behavior. He wants to feel free to talk to other people, both male and female, as Howard the individual—not as Howard and Krista, the unit. Krista has friends. Why won't she go and talk to them? Why can't she be more independent?

Dick's friend, Larry, has just come over to hang out and watch a ball game with Dick. Vicki feels hurt. Wasn't Dick supposed to spend the weekend with her?

She feels as though Larry is taking something away from her, so she goes and sits on the couch and cuddles up to Dick. Larry suddenly feels like an unwelcome intruder, and Dick feels his loyalty being divided. Why does Vicki feel as though she has to compete? Why isn't she sensitive to his relationship with his friend? Why isn't she sensitive to his needs?

THE SMARTEST WOMAN KNOWS . . .

If You Try to Be Everything to a Man, You're Only Going to End Up Feeling Left Out.

———

To Hover Is to Smother.

Myth: A Couple Who Is in Love Shares Everything.

Fact: When You're in Love, You Don't *Have* to Share Anything. You Don't Have to Share Your Food. You Don't Have to Share Every Minute of Your Free Time. You Don't Have to Share Every Thought, and You Don't Have to Share the Same Bathroom.

Myth: A Couple Who Is in Love Shares Everything.

Fact: Real Love Means Being Able to Say, "I Respect Your Separateness."

The Smartest Woman Knows the Difference Between . . .

Being a Couple and Being Someone's Shadow.

Being Accessible and Being Underfoot.

Being Connected and Being Attached at the Hip.

THE SMARTEST WOMAN KNOWS . . .
Men Like Women Who Aren't Buried in Their Past.

Ralph and Carla have been going out for six months, and she really likes him. As she grows to care more about Ralph, Carla is letting him find out more about her life. The problem is that as Ralph finds out more about Carla, he's swiftly reaching the conclusion that she is still totally involved, and often embroiled, with her ex-husband. Carla doesn't see it that way. She knows that she doesn't have any feelings left for her ex-husband, except of course a little bit of anger. But they have the children in common, and consequently they need to talk to one another. Unfortunately these conversations often turn into war zones, and Carla is so upset that she confides her distress to Ralph.

Ralph doesn't understand. He's never been married. When he hears about Carla's fights with her ex, he thinks this kind of thing is going to go on *forever*. Ralph believes these fights indicate that Carla still cares for her ex. By hearing about their battles, he feels as though *he* has become a player in *their* marriage. Sometimes instead of feeling as though he and Carla have a relationship, he feels as though her primary feelings are tied up in her dissolved marriage, and he's just an onlooker. Sometimes this makes him jealous; but even worse, sometimes it makes him feel that he is a child watching Mommy fight with Daddy.

Truth be told, Ralph has a personal history that has its own melodramas. But Ralph and Carla have constructed their relationship in such a way that Carla sees none of his ancient history. Ralph, on the other hand, spends a lot of time at Carla's house with her children, whom he likes. He sees when she answers the phone, whom she talks to, and how she talks to them. Actually, Carla's inner life is nowhere near as chaotic as her outer world, but Ralph doesn't see this.

Carla needs to stop and carefully consider the speed with which she gave Ralph total access to her life. It would be very easy to simply assume that if Ralph were a *real* adult male, he would be able to cope with everything that went on in Carla's past. But that's not a fair assumption. Ralph is serious about Carla, but he's also scared for his future. He has a career that he's serious about, he has interests he wants to pursue, he has things he wants to do. Looking at what he perceives to be the clutter in Carla's house and Carla's psyche, he doesn't see how he will be able to do that. Ralph is very sincere. He would like to be able to be a part of Carla's life, and he would like to be able to have a meaningful relationship with her children. But the messy parts from her past are overwhelming his hopes for the future.

Carla has to realize that she's scaring Ralph. She needs to acknowledge that Ralph's concerns are realistic and practical. She has three jobs to do. First, she needs to start keeping her old business with her ex separate from her new interactions with Ralph. This means keeping necessary phone conversations (as well as any face-to-face interactions) private. Next, she needs to resist the impulse to complain to Ralph about everything her husband is doing now or did in the past. Finally, Carla needs to clean up as much of her past as she can to make more room for her current and potentially future relationship with Ralph. This means pulling the plug on remaining emotional connections she has been unwilling to acknowledge or confront.

THE SMARTEST WOMAN KNOWS . . .
When Two People Are Connected by Anger, They Are Still Very Connected.

The Nicest Guy in the World Can Look at the Most Sympathetic Woman in the World and Wonder What She Did to Make Her Ex So Mad at Her.

Bury a Man in Your Past, and You'll Scare Him Out of Your Future.

THE SMARTEST WOMAN KNOWS . . .

A Narcissistic Man Is like a Plate of Escargots—Very Little Meat and Way Too Much Shell.

An Abusive Man Is like a Lion on the Prowl—Dangerous, Predatory, and Best Left to Himself.

A Hostile Man Is like a Frightened Armadillo—All You Ever Get to See Is His Armor.

A Man Who Can't Make a Commitment Is like a Rooster Who Can't Crow—You Can Never Count on Him to Be There When You Need Him Most.

THE SMARTEST WOMAN KNOWS . . .

If You Love a Man Who Isn't Good for You, the Hardest Thing in the World Is to Turn and Walk Away. But It's Also the Smartest Thing in the World.

Merilee and Carl have been going out for almost a year, and although in some ways they seem to be getting closer and closer, Carl's behavior is getting worse and worse. Merilee *knows* that she loves Carl, but she doesn't feel that she can count on him. She *believes* that Carl loves her, but she *knows* he doesn't genuinely value her. She's not really sure what the problem is. Perhaps it's another woman; perhaps it's the commitment thing; perhaps he drinks too much; perhaps he's so career driven that there's no room for anything else; perhaps he's so involved with himself that there's no room for anyone else; or perhaps he's just plain perverse.

Whatever the reason for Carl's behavior, Merilee's basic needs are not being met. But Merilee is understandably torn. She's already spent so much time with Carl that she doesn't want to throw away the investment of time and love, and she's also terrified of the additional pain she might initially feel from a breakup. Yet the way he has been treating her is causing her profound unhappiness, and Carl doesn't seem to be willing to change.

Many women have found themselves in Merilee's

predicament. When Merilee met Carl, she was very anxious to have love in her life, so she went with the feeling. This is the kind of scenario that makes it all too easy to get caught up in a relationship with another person before either one of you is truly "known" to each other.

When you move quickly at the beginning of a relationship, you can become involved before you fully process a man's drinking habits, his work habits, his issues with fidelity, or his issues with commitment. You take one step and then another, and before you know it you've gone an incredible distance with a man you probably should have walked away from at the very beginning.

Now, like Merilee, you feel as though you have only two choices: Put up with a relationship that provides ongoing grief, or get out. You don't want to continue to live this way, and you know what you have to do. But breaking up with a man you care about is never easy. Here are three steps to help you get started.

1. Make an immediate commitment to *stop* trying to change him.
2. Make a serious commitment to *start* changing yourself.
3. *Find* a therapist, a counselor, a support group, or a twelve-step program to help you find guidance and encouragement.

Breaking away from a serious relationship is a difficult process. If you're not emotionally able to go "cold turkey," don't give up. You can still stop trying to change him, you can still make the commitment to yourself, and you can still find the support to help you change. The Smartest Woman knows that in some situations the only thing you can do is change your own behavior a little at a time until you get the strength you need. Just start moving in the right direction, and for every step you take, no matter how profound the urge, don't question your decision, don't doubt your judgment, and don't look back.

THE SMARTEST WOMAN KNOWS . . .
There's a *Big* Difference Between Playing in the Sand and Burying Your Head in It.

It's Never Smart to Settle for Less than You Deserve.

THE SMARTEST WOMAN KNOWS . . .
Yes, of Course, a Man Likes a Woman Who Doesn't Try to Change Him.

But who cares! There are two excellent reasons why the Smartest Woman never tries to change a man, and they have nothing to do with what *he* likes or dislikes: Reason #1: Nobody changes unless he (or she) wants to. Reason #2: Giving all your energy to a man who needs changing or saving is stealing energy from yourself.

This is important for your future, so pay attention! Use your precious energy in ways that can really make a difference in *your* life. Spend your energy and time on people who want to have better relationships with you. Use your energy to improve situations that can be improved. You can, for example, work on changing yourself; you can devote more time to building better relationships with your children, your family, or your friends. You can devote more time to improving your work situation; you can do a million and one things that will make your life better. So get to it, and let the guy be whoever or whatever he wants to be. If he doesn't genuinely appreciate you and reflect that appreciation by the way he behaves, he hasn't earned your time or your care.

The Smartest Woman Is Energy Efficient. She Saves Her Energy for the People Who Want to Light Up Her Life.

Myth: If You Love a Man Enough (No Matter How Badly He Treats You), Eventually He'll Realize the Error of His Ways and Come to His Senses.

Fact: If You Love a Man Enough (No Matter How Badly He Treats You), Eventually He'll Figure Out a Way to Treat You Even Worse.

Myth: If You Put Up with His Cheating Ways Long Enough, Eventually He'll Realize You're the Only Woman for Him and Come to His Senses.

Fact: If You Put Up with His Cheating Ways Long Enough, Eventually He'll Think You're Giving Him Permission.

Myth: If You Put Up with a Jerk Long Enough, Eventually He'll Realize He's Being a Jerk.

Fact: If You Put Up with a Jerk Long Enough, Eventually He'll Become an Even Bigger Jerk.

THE SMARTEST WOMAN KNOWS . . .

. . . Men Like Women Who Don't Put Up with Their Garbage.

. . . Women Like Themselves Better When They're Not Putting Up with Anybody's Garbage.

The Smartest Woman Knows When She Needs Help, and She Acts on That Knowledge.

You and the "jerk" broke up because his jerkiness was so overwhelming, you couldn't deal with it anymore. But he misses you. So he calls you and pleads. What do you do and what do you say? Well, you don't jump up and down crying with joy, and you don't say yes. Before you decide that the "jerk" has finally turned into the "prince" you always dreamed of, you need to make a commitment to yourself to remain grounded and realistic. This is essential, because if the relationship falls apart again, after you've given it your all, you could be feeling far worse than you're feeling right now. Remember that the Smartest Woman would tell you that the statistics are probably not in your favor. Unless you've both genuinely changed, the relationship will most likely slide back to where it was.

If you're going to again try to have this relationship, the Smartest Woman would tell you that this time you need to have your relationship supervised. That means couples counseling. If you care about this relationship, it is an investment that *both* of you *must* make. This is not a test of *his* intentions. However, his attitude toward entering a counseling situation will give you a fairly good idea of what his intentions really are. Once you see a qualified counselor, you can work together to set up some ground rules for the relationship that will help you build something better between the two of you.

Perhaps you are afraid to talk about counseling. Perhaps you are afraid that if you insist upon it, your partner will see it as a demand, and he will change his mind about you. This kind of thinking is not smart. If he sees it as a demand, he's going to see anything as a demand, and he'd change his mind anyway. Some women want to wait until the relationship gets reconnected before they suggest counseling. Again, this is not smart. At this moment, when *he* is genuinely uncomfortable, you have a little more power in the relationship than you might have under normal circumstances. Use this constructively for both of you. And don't fly into his arms until both of you have expressed what you really want to a qualified third person.

The Smartest Woman would also tell you that this is a very good time for you, as an individual, to be working with a therapist or a support group to be sure that this relationship is really what *you* want for the rest of your life, or even for the next six weeks.

THE SMARTEST WOMAN KNOWS . . .
Whether She Stays or Goes, Getting Help Is the First Step to Getting Healthy.

It's Always Smart to Take Yourself and Your Needs Seriously.

Myth: *It was love at first sight.*

Fact: *It was trouble.* Sometimes the one man you think you *have* to have is the one who doesn't really want you. If his lack of interest is keeping you interested, you need your therapist more than you need this relationship.

THE SMARTEST WOMAN KNOWS . . .

. . . Just Because He Looks like He Has Everything Wired Doesn't Mean He Won't Get Strung Out.

———⚮———

. . . Just Because He Works Out at the Gym Doesn't Mean He Can Carry the Weight of the World on His Shoulders.

———⚮———

. . . Just Because He Looks like a Giant Doesn't Mean He Never Feels like a Little Kid.

———⚮———

. . . Just Because He Wears Big Shoes Doesn't Mean He Feels Confident He Can Fill Them.

———⚮———

. . . Just Because He's Tall Doesn't Mean He Never Trembles . . . Even Men with Big, Strong Legs Get Weak at the Knees.

———⚮———

. . . Just Because He Has Real Presence Doesn't Mean He Can Always Perform.

THE SMARTEST WOMAN KNOWS . . .

Men Like Women Who Know They Have Fears and Anxieties and Don't Hold It Against Them.

What on earth is Peter doing? Suzanne is coming to his apartment for drinks, and right now he looks more like a CIA operative than a man preparing for his fifth date with a woman he really likes. Basically, what he's struggling to do is shred, hide, or disguise anything that disturbs the image he's trying to maintain.

He picks up the bank statement that shows he's into his checking overdraft and hides it in a shoe box in the back of the closet behind the two weeks' worth of dirty laundry, the broken CD player, and the four months' worth of untouched copies of *Time* magazine. He pushes the chair to hide the crack in the wall. He furiously vacuums the dog hair off the couch and hopes the dog won't have another accident. He turns down the volume on his answering machine in case his mother calls with one of her embarrassingly lengthy and over-protective messages.

He tries to arrange all his "cool" books so they are noticeable, and shoves the ones that show questionable taste to the back of the bookcase. Finally, he does a quick check of the walls and removes the picture of him with his ex-girlfriend on last year's skiing holiday. That reminds him to do a quick wallet check for pictures. If she asks to see recent photos of his niece and nephew, he doesn't want his ex's picture to change the mood.

Quickly, he runs through the refrigerator, throwing out the four terrifyingly old eggs, the rotting lettuce, the stale bread, the moldy pasta sauce, and the green bacon. Yikes, what if she has to go to the bathroom? He races to the bathroom, a roll of paper towels in his hand. One, two, three, he picks up the towels, pulls the shower curtain closed, and wipes up all the hair in the sink. He doesn't have any clean hand towels, so he throws the cheerfully decorated roll of Bounty on the sink and drapes a beach towel over the shower railing just in case. Whew! Maybe now he can relax for half a minute if he can just stop worrying about that bank statement in the back of the closet . . . and the meeting at work tomorrow morning.

———— ⛓ ————

The future, cholesterol, bad knees, failing backs, unemployment, the IRS, crime, aging, hostile employers, the uncertainties of self-employment, competitive partners, sales quotas, dependent mothers, bills, bills, bills, problematic siblings, depressed dads, shrinking bank balances, premature ejaculation, waning testosterone, and what's happening in his relationship with you. These are just a few of the things that the man in your life may be thinking about, and not necessarily in that order.

The typical man has gone through a lot of conditioning to make him feel that he should always look as though he has his life together. Even when his stress level is so high that he feels like whimpering in a corner, he will probably try to look and sound as though he knows what he's doing. An unemployed man, for example, will usually try to sound like he's in control of his future. Statistically, the chances are that the man in your life has something he's worrying about. Some of his worries he will probably eventually share; others he may always conceal to some degree.

We are not suggesting that you spend so much time focusing on a man's issues that you spend less time on your own. What we are suggesting is that you learn to look more closely behind the male facade and try to be more sensitive to his human concerns. They are not substantially different from yours.

THE SMARTEST WOMAN KNOWS . . .
Just Because He's Human Doesn't Mean He's Not Desirable.

If You're Waiting to Meet a Guy Who Has It *All* Together, You May Be Waiting Forever.

THE SMARTEST WOMAN KNOWS . . .
Men Like Women Who Know How to Do the Cha-cha.

One, two, cha-cha-cha. One, two, cha-cha-cha. Give, take, cha-cha-cha. Take, give, cha-cha-cha. Move away, move together. Move away, move together. Turn around and kiss. Everyone says that relationships are a dance, but nobody gives us a set of footprints to put on the floor and follow. If you're lucky, you've found a guy with a little bit of rhythm. But if you haven't, you can't be afraid to lead. In a dance that few people understand all that well, most men genuinely appreciate a partner who is out there trying. And the most important place to be dancing your brains out is in the area of communication. *Cha-cha-cha*.

THE SMARTEST WOMAN KNOWS . . .
A Relationship Without Good Communication Is Not a Relationship.

THE SMARTEST WOMAN KNOWS . . .
In a Healthy Relationship, T-A-L-K Is Never a Four-Letter Word.

Sheila and Frederick have it all: six telephones (including two cellulars). A fax machine. Two modems. A ham radio. A satellite dish. With all that equipment, it's hard to believe that they don't communicate—but they don't. That's because there's a big difference between talking to someone and talking *near* someone, *at* someone, *through* someone, or *around* someone. Sheila and Frederick don't understand what that difference is, and many other couples can sympathize and relate all too well to their experience.

Some of us were fortunate enough to have grown up with strong positive relationship role models. We grew up with parents and family members who knew how to talk with each other and take care of their individual needs in a cooperative, successful framework. But many of us were not that fortunate. We come from families who conveyed all the wrong ways to love. These families often had whole repertoires of communication strategies that were as convoluted as they were misguided. If truth be told, many of the individuals in these families didn't even know what they wanted from each other, but even when they did, they didn't have a clear sense of how to get it in a nondestructive, cooperative way.

If you were a child in a family that communicated with ineffectual, unpleasant, or dysfunctional styles, when you begin to have relationships and a family of your own, you have to start all over again. You have to wipe away communication techniques that relied on angry silences, sarcastic tones, humiliating language, barely audible grunts, or confusing body language. You have to replace those methods with a style of interaction that is productive and constructive. You have to learn to be more honest, more open, more direct, and more sensitive.

THE SMARTEST WOMAN KNOWS . . .

• If you don't know how to listen, you don't know how to communicate.

• If you always have to give your opinion, you don't know how to communicate.

• If you always raise your voice to make your point, you don't know how to communicate.

• If you don't let the other person speak, you don't know how to communicate.

• If you always have to have the last word, you don't know how to communicate.

• If you speak to another adult the way you would speak to a small child, you don't know how to communicate.

THE SMARTEST WOMAN KNOWS . . .
Men Like Women Who Know How to Touch with Their Words.

When Sheila and Frederick have a fight, inevitably what they do is scream for about ten minutes. Then one of them stops speaking, and the other joins in the angry silence. This silence typically lasts until bedtime. Since Sheila and Frederick are very attracted to each other, they make up by making love. They both apologize, and it's forgotten for a few days, until they have another fight.

Although this method of crisis resolution has its sexy side, it's not truly resolving anything. Eventually Sheila and Frederick are going to be more accustomed to each other physically and less quickly aroused. One day either Sheila's or Frederick's hormones are going to slow down, and Sheila and Frederick may be too angry to make love. On that day, Sheila and Frederick are going to be stuck with a communication style that doesn't work, and a large assortment of unresolved issues and resentments.

THE SMARTEST WOMAN KNOWS . . .
Making Love and Making War Are Not the Only Two Ways to Make a Point.

———— ⚬⚬⚬ ————

Burying Your Conflicts Under the Sheets Turns a Happy Home into a Haunted House.

———— ⚬⚬⚬ ————

It's Smart to Make Up Before You Make Out.

———— ⚬⚬⚬ ————

Building a Relationship Is like Building a House. You Work on the Foundation Before You Work on the Bedroom.

THE SMARTEST WOMAN KNOWS . . .
Men Appreciate Women Who Push for Better Communication.

Saul really loves Ellie. He says that what he appreciates most about her is that she always makes him talk things through. When they have a problem, she says, "We have to talk about this. I want to hear what you're feeling, and I want to tell you what I'm feeling." And they talk. Not scream. Talk.

———⊷———

Jamal says that what he most likes about Natalie is that he can tell her anything, and he does. When he messes up on the job, he shares his feelings with Natalie because he wants to hear her opinion about what happened.

———⊷———

Dennis says that when he and Maggie were dating, they went to a mall. At the mall they each went their own direction to do their own shopping. On the way back, they stopped at a roadside diner, a real greasy spoon, for a cup of coffee. He says that they started to talk about what they bought and the various little things that happened at the mall. As he puts it, "Suddenly I realized that I could be friends with this woman for the rest of my life. That's when I knew we had to get married."

THE SMARTEST WOMAN KNOWS . . .

Even if He Doesn't Know How to Express It, Every Man Wants the Woman He Loves to Be His Good Friend.

THE SMARTEST WOMAN KNOWS . . .

• There's a Big Difference Between Trying to Manipulate a Man and Trying to Make Him Feel Good About Himself.

• Men Like Women Who Give Them All Kinds of Positive Reinforcement.

April loves it when her boyfriend Jed compliments her. When he tells her how smart she is, she feels great. When he tells her how pretty she is, she feels a little thrill. When he tells her how cute she looks cutting up the veggies for pasta primavera and then tells her how delicious the pasta tastes, she likes it a lot. So why doesn't she realize that Jed likes compliments as much as she does?

Nobody ever taught April or any of her sisters how to compliment men. In fact, April was very subtly discouraged from doing so. When she first started dating, she was too shy and embarrassed to tell a guy what she liked about him. She felt that doing so would make her appear overeager and desperate. Later she came to believe that women who made a practice of complimenting men were manipulative and insincere. So April never learned to say things that might make a man feel appreciated, admired, and liked. That's too bad, because it would really make Jed happy if he thought that April noticed some of his better qualities.

The Smartest Woman Isn't Afraid to Let a Man Know the Things About Him She Finds Special.

THE SMARTEST WOMAN KNOWS . . .

If He Could Read Your Mind, It Would Be Really Scary.

THE SMARTEST WOMAN KNOWS . . .
Men Like Women Who Are Able to Articulate What's Going On in Their Heads.

Leah says Stuart, her fiancé, doesn't communicate, and has absolutely no interest in anything she feels. According to her, she knows this because he's never sensitive to how she feels. Take last week, for example. Simon, Stuart's fourteen-year-old son from his first marriage, was visiting. While Simon and Stuart were doing some male bonding, Leah went shopping. On the way home, she picked up an action adventure video that she thought they all could watch. When she got home, she discovered that Simon and Stuart had already seen it. For some reason, that made her feel weepy. She'd had the kind of week at work where everything seemed to go wrong, and this was one final frustration. Besides, she really wanted Simon to like her, and she didn't seem to be doing anything right. When she got upset, Stuart became annoyed; he couldn't understand why she was making such a big deal out of nothing.

Leah suffers from a syndrome that affects many women, as well as many men. She doesn't always let the people around her know what she is feeling *as it's taking place*. She never said to Stuart, "I really want to try to have a positive relationship with Simon, so I'm going to try to do things that he would like." She never said to Stuart, "My boss is harassing me, so I'm a little edgy from it." She never said anything, so Stuart was not made aware of the *process* she was going through. All he got was the end result—an emotional reaction that seemed extreme.

Like many women, Leah wants Stuart to do the following:

- Make her feel good even when he doesn't know that she feels bad.
- Know what she needs, even when she acts like she doesn't need anything.
- Know what's important to her, even though those things have never been important to him.
- Know what it's like to be a woman, even if he's never watched one single hour of *Oprah*.

The Smartest Woman Knows that the Average Guy Will Never Be Able to Compete with Kreskin.

THE SMARTEST WOMAN KNOWS . . .
A Man Likes a Woman Who Can Tell Him What's Wrong Without Blaming It All on Him.

Many women have a tendency to let their frustration and annoyance build to the point where suddenly it all erupts into a blaming, shaming harangue. You put up with the fact that he's never the one to stop at the store on the way home, make the coffee on a daily basis, take the pet to the vet, or drive to the cleaner's, and then one day it all comes out in a torrent of accusations about his selfishness. Because you let it go so far, he now perceives each of these chores as a demand on him, as opposed to a regular part of life. He wonders, "If I'm so selfish, why is she with me?"

Or, you put up with his flirting at parties, his emotional-distancing techniques, his ambivalence about commitment, his ambivalence about parenthood, his ambivalence about buying a house, or even his cheating, for years. Every few months you go mildly berserk, threaten to leave, and tell him he's the worst man on the planet. He thinks, "If I'm the worst man on the planet, why is she still with me?"

THE SMARTEST WOMAN KNOWS . . .
. . . It's Not Smart to Talk like a Victim.

. . . It's Not Smart to Act like a Victim.
. . . It's Not Smart to Think like a Victim.
. . . It's Not Smart to Save Your Grievances
the Way Some People Save String.

THE SMARTEST WOMAN KNOWS . . .
The Time to Talk About Problems Is When You First Notice Them.

Unlike a good wine, problems do not improve if they are left in the cellar to age. Leave them alone, and little ones become bigger. Leave them alone, and bigger ones become toxic.

THE SMARTEST WOMAN KNOWS . . .
A Problem, like a Weed, Is Most Easily Stopped if You Can Nip It in the Bud.

THE SMARTEST WOMAN KNOWS . . .
Men Like Women Who Know the Difference Between Talking and Judging.

If any of your conversations include phrases such as "I would never do it that way," "That's just like you," or "You never do anything right," then you're not communicating, you're judging.

THE SMARTEST WOMAN KNOWS . . .
. . . Men Like Women Who Know the Difference Between Talking and Criticizing.

Do your conversations include any of the following phrases? "You're the worst." "That's stupid." "Your hair's too short again." "Why do you have such terrible taste?" "Could you just this once not be so cheap?" If so, you're not talking, you're criticizing.

THE SMARTEST WOMAN KNOWS . . .
A Man Likes a Woman Who Doesn't Turn Every Dialogue into a Monologue About Her Needs and Feelings.

Chip says that he can't talk to Julie, because Julie doesn't understand the concept of talking. According to him, when she says "We have to talk about our problems," what she means is "I'm going to tell you how I feel, and I'm probably going to get more upset while I'm doing it." Now, many smart women can identify with Julie. If they could talk to Chip, they would tell him that Julie wants some kind of emotional reaction when she talks about her feelings. And they would tell him that he's not responding in a way that she understands.

But the Smartest Women would also tell Julie that Chip may not understand how to do this. They would watch Julie as she speaks with greater and greater intensity. They would understand that Julie may feel that Chip doesn't truly hear what she is saying. They would recognize that she is probably hoping against hope that eventually Chip will catch on and give her what she wants. Then they would tell Julie that this is an ineffective method that has already failed scores of women.

Here's the problem: Chip probably doesn't get it, and Julie's intensity isn't making it any better. This doesn't mean that Chip is an emotional klutz, and it doesn't mean that he's a bad person; it just means that he can't process Julie's methods, and all he's doing is becoming numb. The Smartest Woman would tell Julie to talk to Chip about how *he* feels instead of just going on and on about how *she* feels. Perhaps together they can find a better way to talk to one another.

THE SMARTEST WOMAN KNOWS . . .

It's Not Smart to Finish Sentences You Didn't Start.

***

If You're Talking More and More, and He's Talking Less and Less, You Need to *Really* Talk.

THE SMARTEST WOMAN KNOWS . . .
Men Like Women Who Don't Whine While They Dine.

Cathi is complaining again, and sometimes to Seth it feels as though that's all Cathi does. To listen to her tell it, she is surrounded by relatives who don't appreciate her, co-workers who don't work as hard as she does, plumbers who don't return her phone calls, and cosmetic consultants who always sell her the wrong shade of lipstick.

Currently Cathi is redecorating her bathroom, and the painter missed a couple of spots. When Seth had his bathroom painted, the guy who did the job painted the window shut so successfully that Seth had to crawl out on the fire escape with a hammer and chisel to get it open. Yet, *he* didn't complain. He's beginning to wonder what it is with this woman and her chronic dissatisfaction. When Seth first met Cathi, he liked her because she was fun, and cute. Then, her stories about her travails seemed charming and sympathetic. Now they just seem tedious.

Cathi doesn't understand what Seth is feeling. As far as she's concerned, she's just sharing information about her life. Her woman friends all seem to like talking to her. They don't complain when she complains. They commiserate and empathize. But Seth has a more traditionally masculine, problem-solving point of view. Seth doesn't understand why Cathi gets so emotional, and he thinks she's overreacting. Nonetheless, he also feels that he should do something about Cathi's problems, and he keeps looking for concrete solutions. At the same time, he's also getting more and more annoyed.

THE SMARTEST WOMAN KNOWS . . .
The Difference Between a Good Whine and Sour Grapes.

———— ∞ ————

Few Men Understand that Complaining Is a Highly Evolved Art Form.

———— ∞ ————

If You're Looking for a Man Who Wants to Hear Your Complaints, Write a Letter to Ralph Nader.

———— ∞ ————

Just Because a Man Loves You Doesn't Mean He Has the Patience to Hear Every Detail About the Small Things that Go Wrong in Your Life.

THE SMARTEST WOMAN KNOWS . . .

Men Like Women Who Can Talk to Them Without Being Accusative, Insulting, or Downright Mean. Every Smart Woman Has a List of "I" Statements That Work and "I" Statements That Don't Work.

"I" Statements That Work:

> I feel hurt, and I want to hear what you feel.
> I feel troubled, and I want to hear what you feel.
> I feel confused, and I want to hear what you feel.
> I feel very vulnerable, and I want to hear what you feel.
> I feel very upset, and I want to hear what you feel.
> I want to understand.
> I want to work this out.
> I want to make it better.
> I want you to tell me what you think is happening, so I can understand.

"I" Statements That Don't Work:

> I think you're *all* wrong.
> I think it's all your fault.
> I think you're a jerk.
> I think you're doing this on purpose.

I think you're confusing me with your mother.

I think your whole family is horrible.

I think you're just like your father, but at least he makes money.

I can't stand the sight of you.

I'm packing.

I'm not listening. . . .

THE SMARTEST WOMAN KNOWS . . .
You Don't Get What You Want by Starting an Argument.

THE SMARTEST WOMAN KNOWS . . .
Men Like Women Who Understand that Everything Has to Be Negotiated.

Gillian, the co-owner of a small boutique, is trying to figure out how to tell her business partner that she needs to take an extra day off during the busy Christmas season. Watch how she goes about trying to get what she wants *and* keep her business partner happy.

1. She decides to bring up the issue when her partner is feeling most relaxed.
2. She initiates a discussion with her soon after she realizes that she needs the day off, so her partner has sufficient time to adjust her own schedule accordingly.
3. She chooses her words carefully so that when she and her partner talk about the issue her partner won't think Gillian is being either unreasonable or demanding.
4. She looks for a *bargaining chip,* something she can give her partner in return so that the sense of equal responsibility for the store is maintained.

As far as her professional life is concerned, Gillian understands that she has to negotiate. But at home, she never takes the time to figure out a negotiating strategy that will work. Let's watch how Gillian behaves at home with her husband, Gary. In this case, Gillian wants to see a movie with a romantic theme that is playing in a local theater. She knows that Gary, who is working on his computer, hates romantic movies, so she's prepared for an argument.

> *Gillian:* I know you never want to do anything I want to do, so I don't know why I'm asking, but do you think you could bring yourself to go to the movies with me tomorrow night?
>
> *Gary:* Could you just let me finish what I'm doing! Besides, if I never want to do anything you want to do, why are you even asking?
>
> *Gillian:* That's just like you. You won't even discuss it. You never want to talk about anything!

Stop right here! This scenario is already becoming too convoluted and is clearly heading for a no-win stalemate. What happened so fast and so wrong? Let's make a list of the things that Gillian did that were, at best, ineffective.

1. *She walked in assuming a mantle of defeat.* If you start out with a negative attitude, you've lost before you've even started.

2. *She was already angry with Gary because he doesn't like everything she likes.* It's all well and good to want your romantic partner to agree with you about everything you like and dislike, but it's not going to happen, so give it a rest and get realistic.

3. *She resents the idea of negotiating with her mate.* Gillian has a mistaken notion that when two people are in love, they automatically are supposed to go along with what the other person wants when the other person wants it.

4. *She wants Gary to read her mind.* Gillian wants Gary to understand that she has this sweet little wish to spend an evening with him in a way that she thinks is romantic. Gary doesn't have a clue that Gillian wants to share something meaningful with him; he thinks she just wants to drag him to a movie he doesn't want to see.

5. *She got angry almost immediately.* Anger is never a good negotiating tool. When Gillian got angry, she started talking about a history of resentment rather than focusing on achieving what she wanted.

6. *Throughout her brief conversation with Gary, she failed to focus on her goal—getting to the movies.* Listen to what Gillian was saying. It was a litany of Gary's faults. This is not the way to get someone to do what you want.

What should Gillian do instead? Well, she should look at how she handled a potential problem with her business partner and go through similar steps. For example:

1. *Gillian needs to pick the right time,* a moment when she and Gary are feeling close and things are going well, and she needs to give him some warning.

2. *Gillian needs to pick the right words.* She needs to tell Gary how much she enjoys being with him, and how much pleasure she gets from doing things together. That's why she wants to go to the movie with him.

3. *She needs to make it clear that she doesn't expect Gary to always bow to her demands,* but that occasionally she would like him to understand and share something that she finds romantic.

4. *She needs to make it clear that she's willing to reciprocate.* Perhaps there is something that Gary would like Gillian to do that she has resisted.

Whether Gillian is aware of it or not, women are always attempting to negotiate their relationships. Too often they are doing it by default, cunning, or tears. The Smartest Woman knows that there are better ways. There are direct, straightforward, fair, and reasonable

negotiating skills that will go a long way toward building successful relationships.

The ideal outcome of any negotiation is what's
called a win/win situation, because both parties are able
to walk away from the bargaining table with something
they wanted. In a romantic setting, there are three potential winners: You, your spouse, and the relationship
you have together.

The Smartest Woman Knows that Nobody Wins
Unless Everybody Wins. She Knows the Difference
Between . . .
- Negotiation and Manipulation.
- Negotiation and Exploitation.
- Negotiation and Confrontation.

The Smartest Woman Knows there Are a Thousand and One Things About Which You and Your Mate Will Probably Disagree.

- You turn the thermostat up, he turns it down.
- He turns the electric blanket up, you pull the plug.
- He leaves the toilet seat up, you put it down.
- You want to leave dirty dishes in the sink overnight, he wants to call the board of health.
- You want the tub scrubbed every time it's used, he says, "Why? It's just water."
- You stack the dishes right side up, he stacks them upside down.
- You buy 100-watt floods, he replaces them with 40-watt misers.
- You try to keep all surfaces clear, he treats his daily newspaper like a collectible.
- He wants to make the bed up every morning, you say, "We're not in the army, what's your point?"
- You let the dog sleep in the bed, he hits the ceiling.
- You want to eat out twice a week, he wants to eat out twice a year.
- He's ready for a new set of tires, you're ready for a brand-new car.

- He thinks you should spend the holidays with his parents because that's what his mother expects, you think you should start establishing some new traditions of your own.

THE SMARTEST WOMAN KNOWS . . .

If a Committed Couple Tells You that They Are in Total Accord About Every Decision They Make, They Are Either Lying to You, Lying to Themselves, or Living in Different States.

At the beginning of a relationship, most women tend to concentrate on the "big" issues. Does he like me? Does he like me enough? Do I like him enough? Are we going to get committed? Typically you're more concerned with whether or not you're going to be taking a vacation together than you are about where you're going to go on this vacation. It's hard for either partner to believe that sometime in the future the two of you could be disagreeing not only on where to go, but on when to go, how to go, and whom to go with.

But as a relationship develops, and as both partners feel more secure with each other, individual differences surface with greater frequency, and seem more and more significant, even when they are absolutely insignificant. This is a good thing. It means that you're both feeling secure enough in the relationship to express your separateness. But it's also a challenge, because these differences have to be negotiated.

The truth is that a healthy relationship is always an ongoing process of dealing with differences. Millions of decisions will have to be made (hopefully one at a time), and they will bring into question everything from individual tastes to critical needs; from your recycling practices to your spiritual practices; from how to slice a tomato to where to send the kids to school; from whose parents to visit for the holidays to which video to rent for Sunday night. Every one of these things needs to be handled in a way that feels fair and constructive. None of that King Solomon "cut the baby in half" stuff. This is where that magic word—compromise—comes in.

The most important thing to remember is this: Compromise is not about right and wrong. It is about decision making by two people with two different points of view. Sometimes your point of view will prevail. Sometimes his point of view will prevail. Sometimes you will both feel like you got what you needed. Sometimes you're both going to feel as though you lost. But if the relationship is fundamentally solid, consider yourself lucky, and write the losses off with your tax return.

The Smartest Woman Knows that She's Not Always Going to Get Her Way.

THE SMARTEST WOMAN KNOWS . . .

Being with a Woman Who Doesn't Listen Is like Living in a Country Where No One Speaks Your Language: It's Very Hard to Feel Understood or Valued.

Jake says he is getting tired of hearing how men never listen to what women have to say. In his relationship, he says, Madeline is the one who never really listens. He says that when he starts talking to her, almost inevitably she remembers some chore she has to finish. He says he feels as though conversations with him are the last thing on her priority list.

From Jake's perspective the scenario goes something like this: They sit down to dinner or coffee, and he starts to speak. Within one sentence, she says, "Oh, just a sec, hon." Then she gets up and runs into the kitchen to get something. Or, she says, "Jake, I really want to hear what you're telling me, but I have to ask you a question first." Or the phone rings, and it's another "Just a sec, hon," and she disappears into the other room on her cordless phone to talk to some friend or business associate for thirty minutes.

Now, a woman would understand that Madeline probably is very busy, very harried, and has a lot on her mind. That's probably why she's not able to pay attention to Jake when he's speaking. But a man has a hard time understanding why every phone call from every stranger seems to get more attention than he does.

THE SMARTEST WOMAN KNOWS . . .

It's One Thing to Watch Television While You Do Your Nails; It's Another to Watch Television While You're Listening to Your Partner.

THE SMARTEST WOMAN . . .

• Doesn't Ask a Question if She Doesn't Have Time to Listen to Her Partner's Answer.

• Doesn't Ask a Question if She Isn't Interested in Hearing Her Partner's Answer.

• Doesn't Ask a Question if She Doesn't Care About Her Partner's Answer.

• Doesn't Give Her Opinion if She Isn't Prepared to Hear Her Partner's Opinion Too.

The Smartest Woman Knows that Keeping the Connection Alive Is More Important than Who Is Right and Who Is Wrong.

When Eileen is positive that she's right, she won't budge until she gets an apology. She isn't speaking to her sister because of something that happened five years ago on her mother's birthday. She's not speaking to her ex–best friend because of something that happened on the phone two years ago. She's not speaking to her next-door neighbor because of an incident over her rose-bushes. And if Eileen keeps heading in the direction she's headed right now, by the end of the evening she is not going to be speaking to the man she loves.

The Smartest Woman Never Gets So Vested in Being Right that She's Willing to Let Her Life Go Wrong.

The Smartest Woman Never Gets So Vested in Being Right that She Can't Say "I'm Sorry. Let's Make Up."

The Smartest Woman Knows that if She Wins Too Often, She Runs the Risk of Losing.

THE SMARTEST WOMAN KNOWS THE DIFFERENCE BETWEEN . . .

- Speaking Her Piece and Screaming Her Lungs Out.
- Touching a Man's Heart and Giving Him Cardiac Arrest.
- Playing Fair and Playing Foul.
- Taking a Position and Taking a Swing.

THE SMARTEST WOMAN KNOWS . . .
Men Like Women Who Fight Fair.

When Michele was growing up, nobody in her family ever raised his voice. People held everything inside. When Michele became an adult, she married Harry, who came from a big, noisy family that had loud verbal disagreements. At first Michele hated Harry's fighting style, but eventually she came to appreciate it. She says that when she stands in the middle of the kitchen and yells, "Hey, this is about me!!!" she feels absolutely liberated.

Brittany came from a more troubled family. Her dad was an alcoholic, and when he got drunk, he became verbally abusive and violent. She has never fully recovered from her terror at hearing a loud masculine voice. If her husband gets angry and speaks loudly, she starts crying almost immediately.

In Dominique's family, her mother was the one who started arguments. She screamed and yelled while Dominique's father quietly tolerated the situation. As an adult, Dominique finds that she also screams—at the children, at her husband, and sometimes at other people who irritate her. She hates herself when she does it, and she feels enormous guilt and shame, but it seems to be almost a built-in, knee-jerk response to stressful situations.

What is your fighting style? And how did it get established? Did you acquire a fighting style from either of your parents? Do you go overboard trying not to do what your parents did? Did you and any of your siblings do battle on a regular basis? Do you come from the kind of family where everything is debated? Do you come from a superpolite family or a no-holds-barred family? Do you come from a family where nobody ever really fought, but everybody sniped? Do you come from a family where verbal assaults were considered humorous or affectionate?

If you fight with your partner the way you fought with your siblings, the way you fought with your parents, or the way your parents fought with each other, it's easy for you to assume that you're fighting fair. After all, it may be the only fighting style you know, so as far as you're concerned that's how people fight. The problem is that very few families handle conflict clearly or cleanly. And that legacy is handed down from generation to generation unless you decide to make it different.

THE SMARTEST WOMAN KNOWS . . .

Just Because Your Family Did It Doesn't Make It Fair.

Just Because Your Family Did It Doesn't Make It Right.

Just Because Your Family Did It Doesn't Make It Smart.

The most important thing to remember is that serious disagreements occur because something needs to be resolved. Your goal is to get to the bottom of a problem that has presented itself. Let's assume, for example, that an argument is taking place because one of you left the car outside with the windows open, and it rained, and the seats are wet.

Try to keep any argument you have focused on the specific event, how to make it better, and how to make sure it doesn't happen again. Keep it in the moment, and talk only about the car, the windows, the rain, and the wet seats. It doesn't help to talk about the history of everything that has ever gone wrong; it doesn't help to talk about other issues, like the garage that needs cleaning, or his wacky sister.

The same kind of logic holds true for big issues. You have to stick with the issue that is presenting itself and resist the powerful temptation to attach to it all the other big problems that you want to talk about.

THE SMARTEST WOMAN KNOWS . . .

No Matter How Angry You Get, It's Never Smart to Fight Dirty.

- Don't Compare Your Partner Unfavorably to Any Other Man.
- Don't Make Your Partner Feel Bad About the Way He Looks, Dresses, Smells, Walks, Speaks, or Snores.
- Don't Make Your Partner Feel Bad About His Earning Capacity.
- Don't Make Your Partner Feel Bad by Pointing Out All the Negative Things Other People Have Said About Him.
- Don't Freeze Your Partner Out.
- Don't Use Tears as a Manipulative Technique.
- Don't Insist on the Last Verbal Swing.

The Smartest Woman Is Always Trying to Find Healthier Ways to Deal with Conflict.

The Smartest Woman Knows the Difference Between Having a Disagreement and Tolerating Abuse.

One of many troublesome factors in abusive relationships is that often the abuse becomes so much a part of everyday life that it is tolerated. Women who live with abusive men frequently find themselves making excuses: "He's not so bad," they say. "It's not as though he gets violent every day, or even every week. It's just once in a while." Or, "It's really my fault. I know how angry he gets when I do something that he doesn't like. I should know better."

As anyone who has ever been in an abusive relationship knows, while you're in the relationship, all the different issues and conflicts may seem overwhelming. Often liquor or substance abuse is involved. A woman may think, "He only becomes abusive when he drinks or does drugs." Sometimes economics are involved, and a woman says, "This started when he lost his job; if he could find work, it would stop." Usually the man is ashamed and apologetic after the abuse occurs, and the woman says, "He promised this would never happen again."

The Smartest Woman's Bottom Line Is This: Abuse Is Abuse Is Abuse. Statistics Overwhelmingly Inform Us that Abuse Intensifies from Incident to Incident. The Sooner You Take Some Kind of Action to Get Help, the Better It Is. Today Is Better than Tomorrow.

THE SMARTEST WOMAN . . .

 . . . Doesn't Chew on Toxic Substances.

 . . . Doesn't Try to Digest More than She Can Stomach.

 . . . *Never* Swallows Her Anger.

THE SMARTEST WOMAN KNOWS . . .
No Matter How Well You Communicate, It's Still Never Smart to Listen to Anyone More than You Listen to the Voice of Your Own Spirit.

When Laura and Eric first started going out, he seemed wonderful—caring, attentive, giving. They have been together for over a year now, and *some* of the time he is caring, attentive, and giving. Other times he is peculiarly controlling, faultfinding, and compulsive. Sometimes she feels as though being with him is an invitation to an immediate headache.

Take last week. Laura had planned this wonderful dinner, but no sooner had she started cooking than Eric started making changes in the menu. She was about to put up the rice, when he told her he wanted pasta. "And, oh," he asked, "instead of baking the fish with vegetables, could you please broil it with lemon?"

Laura was about to make a large salad with three different kinds of greens, when Eric stopped her and said he had just seen a package of frozen green beans, and could he please have those instead. How does Eric know about the green beans in Laura's freezer? Because while Laura was preparing dinner, Eric was busy rearranging the items in Laura's refrigerator. When she asked him what he was doing, he told her he was just trying to be helpful.

The Smartest Woman knows that Laura has a big

problem in the making. In a myriad of ways, large and small, Eric's behavior will always make Laura feel as though she is doing something the wrong way. Too many men engage in this kind of subtle control, and it can be reflected in all of life's little exchanges. For example, you're preparing to go to a cocktail party, and he says, "Why don't you dress up more?" or "Why don't you dress down more?" You're at the party, and he says, "Why are you eating the shrimp instead of the fillet?" You get home from the party, and he says, "Why weren't you friendlier to the Smiths tonight?" Or, "Why were you *so* friendly to the Smiths tonight?" You go into the kitchen to make coffee, and he puts on the news. There is a phone call for him. You answer it. When you go to tell him he's wanted on the phone, he says, "Why are you talking to me now? Don't you understand that I'm doing something?"

Whatever you are doing is *wrong*. That's all you know. Although he always sounds calm, logical, and controlled, you are beginning to sound emotional, hysterical, and out of control. A woman attempting to carve out a relationship with this kind of man is caught in a real dilemma. He's committed, he's faithful, he loves you. But he's making you nuts, and he doesn't seem to understand what he is doing. What do you do?

The Smartest Woman would tell you that, first, you have to come to terms with the fact that there is nothing wrong with what you're wearing, what you're saying, what you're cooking, or what you're doing. This is not about the green beans, or your driving, or anything else you do. This is about control. This kind of man may look calm and collected, but scratch that exterior, and you will find a wellspring of anxiety, anger, or frustration. You didn't cause it, but it can certainly make your life miserable.

If you are involved with a chronic faultfinder, you need to be certain that his behavior is not a prelude to more serious problems. Some men are chronic faultfinders and always seem mildly annoyed about small things. Others may start small, but their behavior heats up— sometimes to out-of-control jealousy, and sometimes eventually to actual physical abuse. Before the relationship progresses any further, you need to start thinking self-protectively.

The first thing for you to do is find some counseling or a support group to help you make choices and keep you from internalizing your partner's faultfinding (this is essential). Then you have four possibilities:

1. Get out of the relationship (which you may not want to do if he's a decent guy who loves you, but who can't stop nagging).
2. Ignore him and just do what you want to do anyway (easier said than done).
3. Fight him on every issue (exhausting, to say the least).

4. Insist on counseling for the relationship (the Smartest Woman's choice).

The Smartest Woman Knows that Women Who Eat Their Anger Have No Room Left for Dessert.

THE SMARTEST WOMAN KNOWS . . .

. . . Trying to Live with an Uncommunicative Man Is Like Trying to Live with a Pet Rock.

Monica is reading an article in a woman's magazine, and she has just reached the point where she is being urged to improve communication in her relationship. "Excuse me!" Monica thinks. Monica doesn't know whether to laugh or cry. No matter how many how-to treatises Monica reads, no matter which techniques she employs, does she think she can get Tony to communicate? Tony is affectionate, Tony is sweet, Tony is good-hearted. But will he talk, genuinely talk? No way.

Of course, Tony talks some. He'll talk about sports, or politics, or work with his friends. Sometimes he even tries to talk to her about sports, or politics, or work. But not many words, and not very often. As for what's happening between them—or anything emotional, for that matter—give us a break!!! Monica says, "Chimpanzees can learn to talk to humans, so I know there's hope for my Tony. I just don't know what to do to make it happen."

The Smartest Woman knows that some men run from their relationships without ever taking a single step out the door. These men hide behind their newspapers, their work, or their hobbies. They are not mean or mean-spirited. They just don't seem to be interested in relating.

Yes, it's true, some men (and for that matter, some women) are scared to death of real intimacy and scared to death of their feelings. Instead of taking this personally, the Smartest Woman takes this where it belongs— to a counselor's office.

THE SMARTEST WOMAN KNOWS . . .
When the *"I Want to Talk About It Now"* Woman Tries to Communicate with the *"If We Don't Talk About It, Maybe It Will Go Away"* Man, a Skilled Professional Will Help Move Things Along.

For Some Couples, It's Going to Take More Than Sophisticated Software to Bring Communication into the 21st Century.

The Smartest Woman Isn't Afraid to Try to Resolve the Problems in Her Relationship.

Andrea and Brad are engaged to be married in six months. As a wedding present, her aunt (who is a therapist) has offered to pay for several sessions of premarital counseling for Andrea and Brad. Not that there are any major problems. But Andrea's aunt believes that every couple benefits from counseling. She says there are specific skills that can be learned and that these skills would benefit Andrea and Brad throughout their marriage.

Andrea loves her aunt, and she appreciates the offer, but she isn't sure she wants to go through with it. Why? Andrea is scared. She's afraid that the counselor will start poking and probing, and perhaps unearth some ambivalence in Brad. She's heard stories of couples who went into counseling and discovered that they didn't want to be married to each other. She's afraid to take that risk.

─── ∞ ───

Cassie and Mitch have both been under a lot of stress lately, and they're not really communicating very well. The difficulties seem to have invaded their bedroom as well. Cassie is afraid to suggest counseling because she's worried that in therapy Mitch will get the courage to reveal to her that he is no longer attracted to her.

— ◦◦◦ —

Donna and Felix have a thousand and one little issues that they don't seem to be able to resolve. Nothing is that important, but they are bickering way too much. Donna honestly believes that they should get a little counseling, but she's nervous. Felix is very dependent on her, and Donna is afraid that therapy will make him aware of this dependency. Suppose he changes? She's afraid he might resolve his dependency issues and leave her.

Many women go through these little internal dialogues every day. They understand the potential benefits of counseling, but they also fear unknown negative consequences. They are filled with questions: "Are both of us ready to confront the reality of our relationship?" "Will something be revealed that he can't handle?" "Does too much personal growth mean having to grow away from the one you love?"

The goal of a well-intentioned couples counselor is to help bring a couple closer together, not to drive a couple apart. But, like everything else in life, couples counseling offers no guarantees. You also should know that there are some therapists who are so dedicated to personal growth that they can put their primary emphasis on you and your partner as individuals rather than on you and your partner as members of a couple. This may not be what you are looking for.

If you feel your relationship could be improved with some therapy, but you are nervous about the possible consequences, the first thing to do is learn more about the therapist or counselor you plan to work with. Before you begin counseling, you may want to have one or two conversations with this therapist about his (or her) orientation and any possible biases. Does she (or he) share your values, for example? You have goals for your relationship. It's essential that whoever you see agrees with these goals. Your partner should have the opportunity to ask the same kind of questions. You need to make sure that you're both comfortable, and that neither of you feels that the therapist's point of view is unfair or overly "male-" or "female-oriented." If your referral was from someone who has worked with this therapist, it would probably be helpful to speak to this person as well. And don't be afraid to shop around. Even the most skilled and respected couples counselor is not a good match for every single couple.

The Smartest Woman Tries to Make Every Decision an Informed Decision.

THE SMARTEST WOMAN KNOWS . . .
Empty Promises Are like Throat Lozenges—
They May Feel Good for a Few Minutes, but the
Pain Always Comes Back.

Jonathan spends all his spare money (and then
some) on his gambling habit. No two ways about it. He
keeps promising his wife, Jenna, that it will stop, but it
never happens.

———— ✦ ————

Greg has made umpteen promises to Hannah that
he will stop or cut back on his drinking. She's still waiting for it to happen.

———— ✦ ————

Jesse acknowledges that he has commitment issues.
He tells Kelly that he loves her, and he promises Kelly
that eventually it will work out, but months have turned
into years, and more years. She wants to get married
before any more years have passed.

———— ✦ ————

Nick is having an affair. His wife, Shannon, found
out because he was careless and left trails of evidence.
When Shannon confronted him, he confessed and
promised that he would end it. In the meantime, he has
also promised his girlfriend, Debra, that he would leave

Shannon. Shannon and Debra are two women with a lot in common.

All these women have the same question: Would a final ultimatum work? The only time such an ultimatum will work is if the man doesn't want to run the risk of losing you. Many women are afraid to find that out. If you're one of these women, the Smartest Woman would tell you that yes, sometimes ultimatums work. And, yes, sometimes they fail. The Smartest Woman would urge you to look at your relationship very closely, and take the following steps before you issue a final ultimatum.

1. *Don't* focus on whether or not he is willing to lose what the two of you have.

2. *Do* focus on whether or not you want to live with this situation for the rest of your life.

3. *Do* make certain that the issue is large enough to warrant such a drastic step. It's silly to say, "Unless you learn to like opera, I'm out of here."

4. *Do* have a real conversation with your partner about what is troubling you, and listen to what he has to say.

5. *Don't* be afraid to hear what he has to say. The truth is the truth. Your fear isn't going to alter what he's doing.

6. *Do* find out what changes he's prepared to make without an ultimatum.

There Are Only Two Times When You Can Issue an Ultimatum to a Man: When You Are Prepared to Back It Up, and When You Are Prepared to Back It Up.

The Smartest Woman Knows that Men Like Women who Cook, Clean, Fluff, and Fold. Why Wouldn't Anyone Like a Partner Who Is Doing All the Work?

The Smartest Woman Also Knows that There Is Nothing Sexier Than the Sight of a Man on His Hands and Knees Scrubbing the Kitchen Floor.

THE SMARTEST WOMAN KNOWS . . .

Just Because He Worships the Ground You Walk on Doesn't Mean He's Going to Offer to Vacuum It.

Scene: The Smythe residence, 10 P.M. on an icy cold Monday night in February. Jim Smythe is watching Monday night football. He's wearing his comfy slippers, and he's munching popcorn. Mary Smythe is standing in the kitchen stacking the dishwasher, staring at an overstuffed Hefty bag. Spot, the family dog, is plaintively trotting back and forth between Jim and Mary. Somebody has to put on a pair of shoes and a coat, put a leash on the dog, and take that painful, lonely walk, first to the Dumpster, and then back and forth, with Spot, on the cold, cold street. Who will it be?

Will it be Mary, because she is the woman, and the woman traditionally assumes more responsibility for domestic chores? (Besides, Spot likes her best.) Or will it be Jim, because garbage removal is often assumed to be a male activity? (Besides, he bought the dog.)

Whoever it will be, *the one thing the smartest woman knows with absolute cer-*

tainty is that <u>nobody wants to take out the garbage.</u>

Here's a rule from the Smartest Woman: *Every couple must find fair ways of sharing household responsibilities.*

Oh yeah, we can hear many of you saying. That sounds good, but it's not the way it works out, even when both partners have full-time jobs. Megan, for example, is one of those women who always seem to be doing more than their share of domestic chores, and she's not even married yet. Nonetheless, her fiancé, Ken, rarely assumes responsibility for any of them.

Because Megan's apartment is larger and more comfortable, she and Ken spend most of their at-home time there. This means that *her* television is the one that breaks from so much use, and *she's* the one who has to take it in to be repaired. *Her* couch is the one that needs shampooing, and she's the one who does it. *Her* dishes are getting dirty, and *her* towels are getting soggy. When Ken leaves, it takes *her* several hours just to straighten up. No question about it, she is spending more time on cleaning, cooking, and laundry than Ken does. Not to mention the time it takes to shop for food to put in the refrigerator so that Ken will always have something to eat.

Megan doesn't know how this happened to her, but it's apparent to anyone who might be watching. She just keeps automatically assuming responsibility for all domestic work without making it clear that she expects fairness. They both come home from work exhausted; Megan says, "Oh, that's okay, sweetie, *I'll* just make us a quick dinner so we don't have to go out." Ken is watching television; Megan says, "Lift your feet, sweetie, so I can sweep up the crumbs." It's Sunday morning, and Ken and Megan wake up; Megan says, "I'm going to get the paper and some rolls. Is there anything else we need?"

A picture is worth a thousand words. Before she starts arguing, Megan should start behaving differently. The first thing Megan must do is to take herself off automatic pilot and stop rushing to do everything. Instead of running to get the vacuum, she could learn this magic question, "What time today (or tomorrow) do you think would be best for the *two* of us to clean the house?" If he absolutely feels he cannot help with household chores, then there is another alternative: hire someone else, and you both split the expense.

The Smartest Woman's Tips for Getting a Man to Do His Fair Share:

1. Don't be afraid to ask. Sometimes he's not pitching in because he's genuinely distracted; sometimes he's not pitching in because he doesn't realize you expect him to help; sometimes he's not pitching in because he doesn't see it as a priority; and sometimes he's not pitching in because he's just feeling lazy, and he figures it's up to you to ask.

2. If he doesn't automatically know where to start or what to do first, assign specific tasks.

3. Get out of his way while he's working and don't act like you're the manager and he's the bumbling employee.

4. Don't feel sorry for him or get angry at him because he doesn't look cheerful or whistle while he works. Ignore any face making.

5. Don't jump in to finish chores for him because he looks so inept and incompetent. Practice makes perfect.

6. Do compliment his work, and don't criticize his failings.

7. Do try to find specific times each week for household cleanups.

8. Just because he loves you, don't let him off the hook.

The Smartest Woman knows absolutely that you will have a better relationship if you avoid traditional male/female role-playing when it comes to doing what has to be done around the house.

THE SMARTEST WOMAN KNOWS . . .
It's Never Smart to Feel Uncomfortable when a Man Is Cooking Dinner.

If You Can't Stop Making Chicken Soup, Start a Catering Company.

Myth: *Men Need to Be Mothered.*
Fact: *To Mother Is to Smother.* Little boys
need mothers; men need partners.

THE SMARTEST WOMAN KNOWS . . .

. . . Men Like Women Who Know the Difference Between a Phillips and a Flat-head Screwdriver.

Becoming totally helpless at the sight of a fuse box isn't sexy. You want a guy who knows how to boil water and fry an egg. That's not asking too much, is it? Well, he wants a woman who isn't rendered powerless in front of a picture that needs hanging. That's not asking too much either.

Besides, nothing is more frustrating than being dependent on a man for minor household improvements. There's no mystery involved in putting up venetian blinds, hanging draperies, or installing a shelf in the bathroom. All you need is an electric drill that you know how to use. And the friendly salesman at your local hardware store will probably be happy to give you the necessary instructions. Once you've learned how to do it, you'll wonder why so many men turn every chore into such a big deal.

THE SMARTEST WOMAN KNOWS THAT MEN LIKE WOMEN WHO . . .

. . . Read Instruction Booklets.

. . . Aren't Afraid of Their VCRs.

. . . Own Electric Drills and Know How to Use Them.

THE SMARTEST WOMAN KNOWS . . .
Empowerment Seminars Cost Hundreds of Dollars; Buying a Five-Dollar Jar Wrench Can Yield the Same Results.

THE SMARTEST WOMAN KNOWS . . .
Men Like Women Who Have a Realistic Attitude About Men and Money.

There are few (if any) relationships that are not touched by money issues. Yet women rarely understand the degree to which most men worry about their finances and their financial status. Historically, men have been conditioned to believe that earning power is an intrinsic part of a man's value. And though times are changing, they still haven't changed enough to take the worry away. Even men who believe in a completely egalitarian relationship acknowledge that the voices of old norms can haunt them: "Can I afford this relationship?" "Is my earning power being judged?" "Do I have enough money to be a desirable partner?" "Will I ever have enough money to be married?" "If I do get married, am I going to have to assume most of the financial responsibility, and will I have the money to do that?"

Now, you may not care all that much about money. Or you may care a lot. Chances are, you fall somewhere in between the two extremes. And, although you may like money, you may not want *his* money. Maybe you're financially independent. Maybe you feel best when you're taking care of yourself. Maybe you feel that your expenses are your responsibility. But it doesn't really matter, because chances are, he's going to worry anyway.

Why are we telling you all this? Just to let you know how serious an issue money is for most men, even those who try to look as though it's not an issue.

The Smartest Woman Knows that Even if He Wants to Treat You Like Royalty He Probably Can't Afford To.

Myth: A Real Man Pays for All the Big Stuff.

Fact: It's a Different World than It Used to Be.
Most Men Can't Afford to Buy the Big
Stuff Any More than You Can.

Outdated standards no longer apply. If he's not automatically picking up all the checks or all the bills, it doesn't necessarily mean that he's cheap, and it doesn't necessarily mean that he's not a good partner. In fact, he may be a better partner than a man who adheres to stereotypical, rigid male-female roles.

Myth: If a Man Really Cares for You, He'll
Spend His Money on You.

Fact: If a Man Really Cares for You, He'll
Spend His Energy on You.

For some men there is nothing easier than plunking down dollars to create the illusion that they are involved. But taking the time to be with you, to listen, to share—that is hard. Any man who is working that hard is showing that he cares.

THE SMARTEST WOMAN KNOWS . . .
Couples Who Don't Resolve Their Money Issues Pay the Price.

In our society, money and power often go hand in hand. This is a big problem for society, but it can be an equally big problem in your relationship if this attitude carries over into the way you deal with each other. Fifty years ago, things were clearer. Pop made the money, and Mom made the roast chicken. Today, nothing about money is clear except for the fact that so many of us never seem to have enough of it, no matter how much we have. He can be earning six figures; you can be earning minimum wage. He can be out of work; you can be giving more to Uncle Sam every month than most people make in a year. You can both be making adequate salaries, or you can both be out of work.

The fact is, whether he admits it or not, someplace in the back of his head the typical guy believes that women judge men by how much they make. Sometimes men respond to this by trying to prove and improve their monetary worth; sometimes they respond to this by getting angry and resentful; and sometimes they respond to this by trying not to be part of this system.

Women, on the other hand, often have equally typical ways of dealing with "the money issue." Often they have been conditioned to feel special and taken care of only if the man is assuming the financial responsibility. Sometimes women respond to this by expecting a man to assume most of the expenses; sometimes women resent financial dependency and want to carry their own weight; and sometimes they try to make their own rules.

Problems about money are most likely to occur when a man and a woman who have differing attitudes toward money and traditional role-playing become involved in a romantic partnership. Compound this with the fact that some men and women believe that money making and decision making go hand in hand, and you can see the kind of basic differences in financial attitudes that can exist between two people.

No matter who makes what, there are dozens of choices about how the two of you handle your money. How you choose to do it is not important. What is important is that neither of you feels cheated, diminished, controlled, used, or abused from the money issues that arise between the two of you. Some basic rules:

THE SMARTEST WOMAN . . .

- Doesn't Get Her Partner into Debt.
- Doesn't Let Her Partner Get Her into Debt.
- Doesn't Judge Her Partner by the Size of His Paycheck.

- Doesn't Judge Her Own Worth by the Size of Her Own Paycheck.
- Doesn't Let Money Mask Bigger Issues.
- Doesn't Try to Control Her Partner with Money.
- Doesn't Let Her Partner Use Money to Control Her.
- Doesn't Act like Money Grows on Trees Unless She Owns an Orchard.

THE SMARTEST WOMAN KNOWS . . .

Bringing Home the Most Bacon Shouldn't Make Anyone the Boss.

THE SMARTEST WOMAN KNOWS . . .

When It Comes to Sex, Everyone Is at Least a Little Bit Different.

———❦———

If You Want to Know What Your Partner Likes, You Can't Be Afraid to Ask Him.

———❦———

If You Want Your Partner to Know What You Like, You Can't Be Afraid to Tell Him.

THE SMARTEST WOMAN KNOWS . . .
Sexual Thoughts Increase in Direct Proportion to the Lack of an Available Partner.

When Carrie and Richie first started having sex together, it was the primary focus of their relationship. It was so incredible! They had sex in the kitchen; they had sex in the living room; they had sex in the shower. Once they even had sex on the balcony, in the middle of December, under a quilt. But that was then; this is now. Carrie and Richie have been married for six years, and sometimes it seems as though they barely manage to have sex in the bedroom.

These days, when Carrie goes out to dinner with her single women friends, sometimes she can't believe how much they talk about sex. Often she feels embarrassed. Not about what they're saying. What embarrasses Carrie is how little interest she has in sex or conversations about sex. Carrie truly loves Richie, and she knows he loves her. They have a very good relationship. And they have two beautiful little girls, whom they both adore. But sex? Carrie says this week sex is about number nine on her priority list of things to do, right after getting the winter clothes out of storage and vacuuming out the car.

Several things worry Carrie:

1. *Is it normal to be so uninterested in sex?*

The Smartest Woman knows that as far as sex is concerned, everyone is different. For some men and women, sex is the primary life focus; others are just as turned on by gardening or golf. Further, in the typical woman's lifetime, she's going to go through many different sexual stages depending upon energy (physical and emotional), hormones, and what else is happening in her life. A young single woman will typically be much more sexually oriented than a young mother who isn't getting enough sleep. And, yes, this is normal.

2. *Even if it's normal, is it a problem?*

The Smartest Woman knows a sexual problem isn't a problem unless it's making someone unhappy. If Carrie's lack of interest is causing stress or tension in her marriage, then it's certainly a problem.

3. *What should Carrie do?*

Talk to her partner. She needs to get some realistic feedback from Richie. It's important for the relationship that Carrie know what he's feeling, and that she's sensitive to those feelings. Has he come to any conclusions about her lack of sexual interest? Does he, for example, feel neglected and need reassurance that she still loves him?

And what about Carrie? Does she need a little more reassurance? Does she need a little more romance or a little more seduction? If so, she needs to find some tender ways of conveying her feelings.

Perhaps Carrie and Richie could do with some marital counseling. Or perhaps all they need is a little more sleep each week, and some time alone. Many couples trying to cope with the demands of work and parenting need to remind themselves that while sex is not everything in a relationship, it shouldn't be neglected. The Smartest Woman knows that often the best sex is not spontaneous sex. Few women really want to think about sex when they're diapering the baby or talking on the phone, and few men are prepared to walk away from the Super Bowl. Maybe Carrie and Richie need to set up a schedule and start putting aside time each week for sexual intimacy. This may not be spontaneous, but it can be very romantic and seductive if both partners are committed.

THE SMARTEST WOMAN KNOWS THAT WHEN
IT COMES TO SEX . . .
- Men Like Women Who Know Their Own
Bodies.
- Men Like Women Who Aren't Afraid to Feel
Sexy.
- Men Like Women Who Don't Keep Score.
- Men Like Women Who Know How to Point.

THE SMARTEST WOMAN KNOWS . . .
Men Like Women Who Know That Being Flexible in Bed Doesn't Mean Being Able to Touch Your Toes with Your Tongue.

Women are often confused about male sexuality and male anatomy. When women watch screen lovers, or read steamy scenes in books, it all seems so easy and perfect. But in reality, it doesn't always work out that way. The Smartest Woman understands that all men are different from one another sexually, and that each man's abilities and desires change over time.

In our sexual fantasies, of course, everything is always touched with magic. Sometimes sexual reality is too. But at other times, sex can become complicated and less than ideal, and both partners have to stay sensitive and flexible. The Smartest Woman knows this and understands that affection, love, commitment, and a little bit of shared humor will do more for a relationship over time than even the most exotic foreplay.

THE SMARTEST WOMAN KNOWS . . .
Real Sex Involves Real Body Parts (Parts That Don't Always Work Perfectly and Sometimes Don't Work at All).

THE SMARTEST WOMAN KNOWS . . .
Men Like Women Who Know What Intimacy Is Before They Start Asking for It.

Intimacy. We say we want it. We say we need it. But there is a big difference between pushing for intimacy and knowing how to be intimate. When you say you want a more intimate connection with the man you love, what is it that you mean? Are you asking for more attention, more time, more loving words, more physical contact, more sex, more time on the town, more time alone? Do you want more trust, more honesty, more communication, or more sharing?

Every woman seems to have her own personal understanding of what an intimate relationship might look like and feel like for her. But too often a woman will talk about intimacy as if it is something she should be getting from a man. Often she doesn't fully recognize that intimacy requires two partners, and she is one of those partners.

She wants to be trusted yet she doesn't fully trust. She wants her partner to be fully forthcoming about his feelings, yet there are many things that she keeps secret. She wants to know everything about his finances, yet, on the advice of her mother, she maintains a hidden bank account. She wants to be able to comfort him when he is sick, yet she tends to play the martyr around her physical discomforts. She wants to have more intimate sexual contact, but she wants it only when she is in the mood. She wants him to be more accepting, yet she often finds herself judging him.

We all want intimacy, but most of us are also scared of it. Intimacy means revealing yourself to another human being. It means being vulnerable to that person. It means opening yourself up in ways that may not be easy or comfortable. The Smartest Woman commits herself to uncovering, examining, and dismantling her own resistance to intimacy before she shifts her focus to what her partner isn't giving her.

THE SMARTEST WOMAN KNOWS . . .
Intimacy Develops Slowly. It Takes a Long Time for Two People to Feel Comfortable Sharing the Same Towel, Let Alone the Same Toilet.

THE SMARTEST WOMAN KNOWS . . .

Commitment Is a Process, Not a Piece of Paper.

The Smartest Woman knows that being in a committed relationship doesn't necessarily mean being married; it doesn't mean having a house with a white picket fence; it doesn't mean being draped in precious jewels by the one you love; and it doesn't mean being joined at the hip. The Smartest Woman knows that making a commitment means making a commitment to working—to working things out and working things through. Making a commitment means making compromises, and it means surviving the loss of fantasies while you slug out the realities of everyday life with another human being who doesn't always have your wants, your needs, your fears, your dreams, your attitude, your internal thermostat, or your sleep schedule.

Not terribly romantic at times. This we know. But real. And meaningful. And special. And very smart.

SEVEN SIMPLE TRUTHS FOR THE SMARTEST WOMAN

1. TREAT A MAN LIKE HE'S A CREATURE FROM ANOTHER PLANET, AND HE'LL ACT LIKE A CREATURE FROM ANOTHER PLANET.

2. BEING IN LOVE CAN FEEL FRIGHTENING, BUT THAT'S NO REASON TO RUN AWAY.

3. COMMITMENT IS NOT A RING, A VOW, A WORD, OR A PROMISE; IT IS A PROCESS.

4. FINDING A RELATIONSHIP DOESN'T MEAN FINDING THE ANSWER; HAVING A MAN IN YOUR LIFE IS AT LEAST AS CHALLENGING AS *NOT* HAVING A MAN IN YOUR LIFE (AND SOMETIMES MORE).

5. A GOOD RELATIONSHIP IS HARD WORK; A BAD RELATIONSHIP IS TOO MUCH WORK.

6. IF YOU CAN'T TOLERATE SEPARATENESS, YOU'RE GOING TO HAVE A HARD TIME NEGO-TIATING TOGETHERNESS.

7. IF YOU LET YOUR RELATIONSHIPS POLARIZE INTO TRADITIONAL MASCULINE-FEMININE ROLES, YOU'LL NEVER GET THE REAL RELA-TIONSHIP YOU DESERVE.